David Mamet
Plays: 3

Glengarry Glen Ross, Prairie du Chien,
The Shawl, Speed-the-Plow

Glengarry Glen Ross is 'a chillingly funny indictment of a world in which you are what you sell . . . You won't hear much better dialogue on the London stage than you get in David Mamet's *Glengarry Glen Ross*. The play is filled with the spiralling obscenity and comic bluster of real estate salesmen caught off-guard; yet underneath that there is fear and desperation.' *Guardian*
'Nobody alive writes better American . . . ̶ ̶ ̶ ̶ ̶ ̶ ̶ ̶ ̶ ̶ carving characters out of language, is a play with real muscle.'

In *Prairie du Chien* a railway carriage spe̶ ̶ ̶ ̶ ̶ ̶ the setting for a violent story of obsessiv̶ ̶ ̶ ̶ ̶ within shooting distance of a card-hustl̶ ̶ ̶ ̶ clairvoyant wondering whether to chea̶ ̶ ̶ ̶ inheritance.
'The concerns of *Prairie du Chien* and *The* ̶ ̶ ̶ ̶ ̶ values exist? Is the world a jungle only? And how, finally, can we know the answer to that or anything else? Big general questions but dramatised with a succinctness, a concreteness, an energy, a fizz and a snap of which few if any playwrights are capable, on either side of the pond.' *New Statesman*

Speed-the-Plow: 'A brilliant black comedy, a dazzling dissection of Hollywood cupidity and another tone poem by our foremost master of the language of moral epilepsy . . . On its deepest level it belongs with the darker disclosures of movie biz pathology like Nathanael West's *The Day of the Locust* and F. Scott Fitzgerald's *The Last Tycoon*. In a sense *Speed-The-Plow* distills all of these to a stark quintessence; there's hardly a line in it that isn't somehow insanely funny or scarily insane . . . a scathingly comic play.' *Newsweek*

David Mamet was born in Chicago in 1947. He studied at Goddard College, Vermont (where he was later Artist-in-Residence), and at the Neighborhood Playhouse School of Theater in New York. His first and many subsequent plays were first performed by the St Nicholas Theater Company, Chicago, of which he was a founding member and Artistic Director. In 1978 he became Associate Artistic Director of the Goodman Theater, Chicago, where *American Buffalo* had been first staged in 1975, subsequently winning an Obie Award and opening on Broadway in 1977 and at the National Theatre, London in 1978. *Sexual Perversity in Chicago* and *Duck Variations* (Regent Theatre, 1977), *A Life In The Theatre* (Open Space, 1979), *Glengarry Glen Ross* (National Theatre, 1983; Pulitzer Prize for Drama 1984), *Edmond* (Royal Court, 1985), *Oleanna* (Royal Court and Duke of York's Theatre, 1993) and *The Cryptogram* (Ambassadors Theatre, 1994) have also been staged in London. Other plays include *Reunion, The Woods, The Water Engine* (all first staged in 1977), *Lakeboat* (1982) and *The Disappearance of the Jews* (1983). For the cinema he wrote the screenplays for *The Postman Always Rings Twice, The Verdict, House of Games, The Untouchables, Things Change* (written with Shel Silverstein), *Glengarry Glen Ross, We're No Angels, Hoffa, The Deer Slayer, High and Low* and *Ace in the Hole*.

by the same author

American Buffalo
The Cryptogram
Dark Pony
The Disappearance of the Jews
Duck Variations
Edmond
Glengarry Glen Ross
Lakeboat
A Life in the Theatre
Mr Happiness
Oleanna
Reunion
Sexual Perversity in Chicago
The Shawl *and* Prairie du Chien
Speed-the-Plow
Squirrels
The Water Engine
The Woods

Screenplays

Glengarry Glen Ross
Hoffa
House of Games
The Postman Always Rings Twice
Things Change (written with Shel Silverstein)
The Untouchables
The Verdict
We're No Angels

Fiction and Non-Fiction

The Cabin
On Directing Film
Some Freaks
The Village
Writing in Restaurants

Poetry

The Blood Chit

For Children

The Owl (written with Lindsay Crouse)
Warm and Cold (drawings by Donald Sultan)

DAVID MAMET

Plays: 3

Glengarry Glen Ross
Prairie du Chien
The Shawl
Speed-the-Plow

METHUEN CONTEMPORARY DRAMATISTS

8 10 9

Methuen Drama
A & C Black Publishers Limited
38 Soho Square
London W1D 3HB
www.acblack.com

This collection first published in Great Britain in 1996
by Methuen Drama

Glengarry Glen Ross was first published in Great Britain in 1984 by Methuen
London, copyright © 1984, 1996 by David Mamet
Prairie du Chien was first published in Great Britain with *The Shawl* in 1989 by
Methuen Drama
Prairie du Chien copyright © 1985, 1989, 1996 by David Mamet
The Shawl copyright © 1985, 1989, 1996 by David Mamet
Speed-the-Plow was first published in Great Britain in 1988 by Methuen
Drama, copyright © 1985, 1986, 1987, 1988, 1996 by David Mamet
This collection copyright © 1996 by Methuen Drama

The author has asserted his moral rights

ISBN-10: 0–413–68750–3
ISBN-13: 978–0–413–68750–0

A CIP catalogue record for this book is available from the British Library

Typeset by Wilmaset Ltd, Birkenhead, Wirral
Printed and bound in Great Britain by Cox & Wyman Ltd, Reading,
Berkshire

Caution

Contents

Chronology   vii

GLENGARRY GLEN ROSS   1

PRAIRIE DU CHIEN   67

THE SHAWL   87

SPEED-THE-PLOW   119

David Mamet:
A Chronology

PLAYS	USA	UK
Duck Variations, St Nicholas Theater Company, Chicago, 1972; Regent Theatre, London, 1977	1972	1977
Sexual Perversity in Chicago, Organic Theater Co., Chicago, 1974; Regent Theatre, London, 1977	1974	1977
Squirrels, St Nicholas Theater Company, Chicago, 1974; King's Head Theatre, London, 1993	1974	1993
American Buffalo, Goodman Theater Company, Chicago, 1975; National Theatre, London, 1978	1975	1978
Reunion, St Nicholas Theater Company, Chicago, 1976	1976	
The Woods, St Nicholas Theater Company, Chicago, 1977	1977	
The Water Engine, St Nicholas Theater Company, Chicago, 1977; Hampstead Theatre, London, 1989	1977	1989
A Life in the Theatre, Goodman Theater, Chicago; Theatre de Lys, New York, 1977; Brighton, 1989	1977	1989
Mr Happiness, New York Shakespeare Festival, New York, 1978	1978	
Prairie du Chien, National Public Radio, 1979; Royal Court Theatre Upstairs, London, 1986	1979	1986
Lakeboat, Court Street Theater, Milwaukee Rep, Milwaukee, WI, 1980	1980	
Edmond, Goodman Theater, Chicago, 1982; Royal Court Theatre, London, 1985	1982	1985
The Disappearance of the Jews, Goodman Theater, Chicago, 1983	1983	
Glengarry Glen Ross, Goodman Theater, Chicago, 1984; National Theatre, London, 1983	1984	1983

The Shawl, Goodman Theater, Chicago, 1985;   1985   1986
Royal Court Theatre Upstairs, London, 1986

Speed-the-Plow, Lincoln Center Theater at the   1988   1989
Royale Theater, Broadway, New York, 1988;
National Theatre, London, 1989

Oleanna, American Repertory Theater,   1992   1993
Massachusetts, 1992; Orpheum Theater, New
York, 1992; Royal Court Theatre, London, 1993;
The Duke of York's, London, 1993

The Cryptogram, Ambassadors Theatre, London,   1995   1994
1994; American Repertory Theater,
Massachusetts, 1995; Westside Theater, New
York, 1995

An Interview (in *Death-Defying Acts*), Variety Arts   1995
Theater, off-Broadway, New York, 1995

SCREENPLAYS

The Postman Always Rings Twice   1981

The Verdict   1982

The Untouchables   1987

House of Games, written and directed by David   1987
Mamet

Things Change, directed by David Mamet, written   1988
by David Mamet and Shel Silverstein

We're No Angels   1989

Homicide, written and directed by David Mamet   1991

Glengarry Glen Ross, directed by James Foley   1992

Hoffa   1992

Oleanna, written and directed by David Mamet   1994

Glengarry Glen Ross

Always be closing.

— Practical sales maxim

This play is dedicated to Harold Pinter

Glengarry Glen Ross was first presented in the Cottesloe auditorium of the National Theatre, London, on 21 September 1983 with the following cast:

Shelly Levene, *fifties*   Derek Newark
John Williamson, *forties*   Karl Johnson
Dave Moss, *fifties*   Trevor Ray
George Aaronow, *fifties*   James Grant
Richard Roma, *forties*   Jack Shepherd
James Lingk, *forties*   Tony Haygarth
Baylen, *forties*   John Tams

Directed by Bill Bryden
Designed by Hayden Griffin
Lighting by Andy Phillips
Sound by Caz Appleton

The US première of the play took place at the Goodman Theater of the Arts Institute of Chicago in a Chicago Theater Groups Inc. production on 6 February 1984 with the following cast:

Shelly Levene   Robert Prosky
John Williamson   J. T. Walsh
Dave Moss   James Tolkan
George Aaronow   Mike Nussbaum
Richard Roma   Joe Mantegna
James Lingk   William L. Peterson
Baylen   Jack Wallace

Directed by Gregory Mosher

Glengarry Glen Ross opened on Broadway at the John Golden Theater on 25 March 1984, presented by Elliot Martin, the Shubert Organization, Arnold Berhard and the Goodman Theater. The cast was as follows:

Shelly Levene	Robert Prosky
John Williamson	J. T. Walsh
Dave Moss	James Tolkan
George Aaronow	Mike Nussbaum
Richard Roma	Joe Mantegna
James Lingk	Lane Smith
Baylen	Jack Wallace

Directed by Gregory Mosher
Lighting by Kevin Rigdon
Costumes by Nan Cibula
Sets by Michael Merritt

The three scenes of Act One take place in a Chinese restaurant.
Act Two takes place in a real estate office.

Author's Note

David Mamet himself worked for a while in a real estate office in 1969. Here are his comments describing that time.

The office was a fly-by-night operation which sold tracts of undeveloped land in Arizona and Florida to guillible Chicagoans. The firms advertised on radio and television and their pitch was to this effect: 'Get in on the ground floor . . . Beautiful home-sites in scenic/historic Arizona/Florida. For more information call . . . for our beautiful brochure.' Interested viewers would telephone in for the brochure and their names and numbers were given to me. My job was to call them back, assess their income and sales susceptibility, and arrange an appointment with them for one of the office salesmen.

This appointment was called a *lead* – in the same way that a clue in a criminal case is called a *lead* – i.e. it may lead to the suspect, the suspect in this case being a *prospect*. It was then my job to gauge the relative worth of these leads and assign them to the salesforce. The salesmen would then take their assigned leads and go out on the appointments, which were called *sits* . . . i.e. a meeting where one actually *sits down* with the prospects . . .

So that's the background to the play. We are in a real estate office. There is a sales contest near its end. The four salesmen have only several more days to establish their position on the sales graph, the *board*. The top man wins a Cadillac, the second man wins a set of steak knives, the bottom two men get fired. The competition centers around the *leads*, with each man trying desperately to get the best ones.

Act One

Scene One

A booth at a Chinese restaurant, **Williamson** *and* **Levene** *are seated at the booth.*

Levene John . . . John . . . John. Okay. John. John. Look: (*Pause.*) The Glengarry Highland's leads, you're sending Roma out. Fine. He's a good man. We know that he is. He's fine. All I'm saying, you look at the *board*, he's throwing . . . wait, wait, wait, he's throwing them *away*, he's throwing the leads away. All that I'm saying, that you're wasting leads. I don't want to tell you your *job*. All that I'm saying, things get *set*, I know they do, you get a certain *mindset* . . . A guy gets a reputation. We know how this . . . all I'm saying, put a *closer* on the job. There's more than one man for the . . . Put a . . . wait a second, put a *proven man out* . . . and you watch, now *wait* a second – and you watch your *dollar* volumes . . . You start closing them for *fifty* 'stead of *twenty-five* . . . you put a *closer* on the . . .

Williamson Shelly, you blew the last . . .

Levene No. John. No. Let's wait, let's back up here, I did . . . will you please! Wait a second. Please. I didn't 'blow' them. No. I didn't 'blow' them. No. One kicked *out*, one I *closed* . . .

Williamson . . . you didn't close . . .

Levene . . . I, if you'd *listen* to me. Please. I *closed* the cocksucker. His '*ex*', John, his *ex*, *I* didn't know he was married . . . he, the *judge* invalidated the . . .

Williamson Shelly . . .

Levene ... and what is that, John? What? Bad *luck*. That's all it is. I pray in your *life* you will never find it runs in streaks. That's what it does, that's all it's doing. Streaks. I pray it misses you. That's all I want to say.

Williamson (*pause*)   What about the other two?

Levene   What two?

Williamson   Four. You had four leads. One kicked out, one the *judge*, you say ...

Levene ... you want to see the court records? John? Eh? You want to go down ...

Williamson ... no ...

Levene ... do you want to go down-*town* ...?

Williamson ... no ...

Levene ... then ...

Williamson ... I only ...

Levene ... then what is this 'you *say*' shit, what is that? (*Pause*.) What is that ...?

Williamson   All that I'm saying ...

Levene   What is this 'you *say*'? A deal kicks out ... I got to *eat*. *Shit*, Williamson ... *Shit You*, Moss ... Roma ... look at the *sheets* ... look at the *sheets*. Nineteen *eighty*, eighty-*one* ... eighty-*two* ... six months of eighty-two ... who's there? Who's up there?

Williamson   Roma.

Levene   Under him?

Williamson   Moss.

Levene   Bull*shit*. John. Bull*shit*. April, September 1981. It's *me*. It isn't *fucking* Moss. Due respect, he's an *order* taker, John. He *talks*, he talks a good game, look at the *board*, and it's *me*, John, it's me ...

Williamson   Not lately it isn't.

Levene Lately kiss my ass lately. That isn't how you build an org ... talk, talk to Murray. Talk to Mitch. When we were on Peterson, who paid for his fucking *car*? You talk to him. The *Seville* ... ? He came in, 'You bought that for me Shelly.' Out of *what*? Cold *calling*. *Nothing*. Sixty-*five*, when we were there, with Glen Ross *Farms*? You call 'em down-town. What was that? *Luck*? That was 'luck'? *Bullshit*, John. You're luck – burning my ass, I can't get a fucking *lead* ... you think that was luck. My stats for those years? Bull*shit* ... over that period of time ... ? Bull*shit*. It wasn't luck. It was *skill*. You want to throw that away, John ... ? You want to throw that away?

Williamson It isn't me ...

Levene ... it isn't you ... ? Who *is* it? Who is this I'm talking to? I need the *leads* ...

Williamson ... after the thirtieth ...

Levene Bull*shit* the thirtieth, I don't get on the board the thirtieth, they're going to can my ass. I need the leads. I need them now. Or I'm gone, and you're going to miss me, John, I swear to you.

Williamson Murray ...

Levene ... you *talk* to Murray ...

Williamson I have. And my job is to marshall those leads ...

Levene Marshall the leads ... marshall the leads? What the fuck, what bus did *you* get off of, we're here to fucking *sell*. *Fuck* marshalling the leads. What the fuck talk is that? What the fuck talk is that? Where did you learn that? In school ... ? (*Pause.*) That's 'talk', my friend, that's 'talk'. Our job is to *sell*. I'm the *man* to sell. I'm getting garbage. (*Pause.*) You're giving it to me, and what I'm saying is it's *fucked*.

Williamson You're saying that I'm fucked.

Levene Yes. (*Pause.*) I am. I'm sorry to antagonize you.

Williamson Let me ...

Levene ... and I'm going to get bounced and you're ...

Williamson ... let me ... are you listening to me ...?

Levene Yes.

Williamson Let me tell you something, Shelly. I do what I'm hired to do. I'm ... wait a second. I'm *hired* to watch the leads. I'm given ... hold on, I'm given a *policy*. *My* job is to *do that*. What I'm *told*. That's it. You, wait a second, *anybody* falls below a certain mark I'm not *permitted* to give them the premium leads.

Levene Then how do they come up above that mark? With *dreck* ...? That's *nonsense*. Explain this to me. Cause it's a waste, and it's a stupid waste. I want to tell you something ...

Williamson You know what those leads cost?

Levene The premium leads. Yes. I know what they cost. John. Because I, *I* generated the dollar revenue sufficient to *buy* them. Nineteen senny-*nine*, you know what I made? Senny-*Nine*? Ninety-six thousand dollars. John? For *Murray* ... For *Mitch* ... look at the sheets ...

Williamson Murray said ...

Levene *Fuck* him. *Fuck* Murray. John? You know? You tell him I said so. What does *he* fucking know? He's going to have a 'sales' contest ... you know what our sales contest used to be? *Money*. A *fortune*. Money lying on the ground. Murray? When was the last time *he* went out on a sit? Sales contest? It's *laughable*. It's cold out there now, John. It's tight. Money is *tight*. This ain't sixty-five. It ain't. It just ain't. See? See? Now, I'm a good *man* – but I need a ...

Williamson Murray said ...

Levene John. John ...

Williamson Will you please wait a second. Shelly. Please. Murray told me: The hot leads ...

Levene ... ah, *fuck* this ...

Williamson The . . . Shelly . . . ? (*Pause.*) The hot leads are assigned according to the board. During the contest. *Period.* Anyone who beats fifty per . . .

Levene That's fucked. That's fucked. You don't look at the fucking *percentage*. You look at the *gross* . . .

Williamson Either way. You're out.

Levene I'm out.

Williamson Yes.

Levene I'll tell you why I'm out. I'm *out*, you're giving me toilet paper. John. I've *seen* those leads. I saw them when I was at Homestead, we pitched those cocksuckers Rio Rancho nineteen sixty-*nine* they wouldn't buy. They couldn't buy a fucking *toaster*. They're *broke*, John. They're cold. They're deadbeats, you can't judge on that. Even so. Even so. Alright. Fine. Fine. Even so. I go in, FOUR FUCKING LEADS they got their money in a *sock*. They're fucking *Polacks*, John. Four leads. I close two. *Two*. Fifty per . . .

Williamson . . . they kicked out . . .

Levene They *all* kick out. You run in *streaks*, pal. *Streaks.* I'm . . . I'm . . . don't look at the *board*, look at *me*. Shelly Levene. *Anyone. Ask* them on Western. Ask Getz at Homestead. Go ask Jerry Graff. You know who I am . . . I NEED A SHOT. I got to get on the fucking board. Ask them. *Ask* them. Ask them who ever picked up a check I was flush. Moss, Jerry Graff, Mitch himself . . . Those guys *lived* on the business I brought in. They *lived* on it . . . and so did Murray, John. You were here you'd of benefitted from it too. And now I'm saying this. Do I want charity? Do I want *pity*? I want *sits*. I want leads don't come right out of a *phonebook*. Give me a lead hotter than that, I'll go in and close it. Give me a chance. That's all I want. I'm going to *get* up on that fucking board and all I want is a chance. It's a *streak* and I'm going to turn it around. (*Pause.*) I need your help. (*Pause.*)

Williamson I can't do it, Shelly.

Pause.

Levene Why?

Williamson The leads are assigned randomly ...

Levene *Bullshit, Bullshit,* you assign them ... What are you *telling* me?

Williamson ... apart from the top men on the contest board.

Levene Then put me on the board.

Williamson You start closing again, you'll *be* on the board.

Levene I can't close these leads, John. No one can. It's a joke. Look, look: you put me in with Roma – we'll go out together, him and me, we'll doubleteam 'em ...

Williamson Dream on.

Levene Okay. Okay ... Just ... (*Pause.*) John, look: just give me a hot lead. Just give me two of the premium leads. As a 'test', alright? As a 'test'. And I promise you ...

Williamson I can't do it, Shel ...

Levene I'll give you ten per cent.

Pause.

Williamson Of what?

Levene Of my end what I close.

Williamson And what if you don't close?

Levene I *will* close.

Williamson What if you *don't* close ... ?

Levene I *will* close.

Williamson What if you *don't*? Then I'm *fucked.* You see ... ? Then it's *my* job. That's what I'm *telling* you.

Levene I *will* close. John, John, ten per cent. I can get hot. You *know* that ...

Williamson Not lately you can't ...

Levene Fuck that. That's defeatist. Fuck that. Fuck it . . . Get on my side. *Go* with me. Let's *do* something. You want to run this office, *run* it.

Williamson Twenty per cent.

Pause.

Levene Alright.

Williamson And fifty bucks a lead.

Levene John . . . (*Pause.*) Listen. I want to talk to you. Permit me to do this a second. I'm older than you. A man acquires a reputation. On the street. What he does when he's *up*, what he does otherwise . . . I said 'ten', you said 'no'. You said 'twenty'. I said 'fine', I'm not going to fuck with you, how can I beat that, you tell me? . . . Okay. Okay. We'll . . . Okay. Fine. We'll . . . Alright, twenty per cent, and fifty bucks a lead. That's fine. For now. That's fine. A month or two we'll talk. A month from now. Next month. After the thirtieth. (*Pause.*) We'll talk.

Williamson What are we going to say?

Levene No. You're right. That's for later. We'll talk in a month. What have you got? I want two sits. Tonight.

Williamson I'm not sure I have two.

Levene I saw the board. You've got *four* . . .

Williamson (*snaps*) I've got *Roma*. Then I've got Moss . . .

Levene *Bullshit.* They ain't been in the office yet. Give 'em some stiff. We have a deal or not? Eh? Two sits. The Des Plaines. Both of 'em, six and ten, you can do it . . . six and ten . . . eight and eleven, I don't give a shit, you set 'em up? Alright? The two sits in Des Plaines.

Williamson Alright.

Levene Good. Now we're talking.

Pause.

Williamson A hundred bucks.

Pause.

Levene Now? (*Pause.*) *Now?*

Williamson Now. (*Pause.*) Yes ... *When?*

Levene Ah, *shit*, John ...

Pause.

Williamson I wish I could.

Levene You fucking asshole ... (*Pause.*) I haven't got it.
(*Pause.*) I haven't got it, John. (*Pause.*) I'll pay you
tomorrow. (*Pause.*) I'm coming in here with the sales, I'll pay
you *tomorrow.* (*Pause.*) I haven't *got* it, when I pay, the *gas* ...
I get back to the hotel, I'll bring it in tomorrow.

Williamson Can't do it.

Levene I'll give you thirty on them now, I'll bring the rest
tomorrow. I've got it at the hotel. (*Pause.*) John? (*Pause.*) We
do that, for chrissake?

Williamson No.

Levene I'm asking you. As a favor to me? (*Pause.*) John.
(*Long Pause.*) John: my *daughter* ...

Williamson I can't do it, Shelly.

Levene Well, I want to tell you something, fella, wasn't
long I could pick up the phone, call *Murray* and I'd have your
job. You know that? Not too *long* ago. For what? For *nothing.*
'Mur, this new kid burns my ass.' 'Shelly, he's out.' You're
gone before I'm back from lunch. I bought him a trip to
Bermuda once ...

Williamson I have to go ... (*He gets up.*)

Levene Wait. Alright. Fine. (*He starts going in his pockets for
money.*) The one. Give me the lead. Give me the one lead. The
best one you have.

Williamson I can't split them.

Pause.

Levene Why?

Williamson Because I say so.

Levene (*pause*) Is that it? Is that *it*? You want to do business that way ...?

Williamson *gets up, leaves money on the table.*

Levene You want to do business that way ...? Alright. Alright. Alright. Alright. What is there on the other list ...?

Williamson You want something off the B list?

Levene *Yeah.* Yeah.

Williamson Is that what you're saying?

Levene That's what I'm saying. Yeah. (*Pause.*) I'd like something off the other list. Which, very least, that I'm entitled to. If I'm still *working* here which for the moment I guess that I am ... (*Pause.*) What? I'm sorry I spoke harshly to you.

Williamson That's alright.

Levene The deal still stands, our other thing.

Williamson *shrugs; starts out of the booth.*

Levene Good. Mmm. I, you know, I left my wallet back at the hotel. Alright. Mmm. (*Pause.*) Mmm ... Fine.

Scene Two

A booth at the restaurant. **Moss** *and* **Aaronow** *seated. After the meal.*

Moss Polacks and deadbeats.

Aaronow ... Polacks ...

Moss Deadbeats *all*.

Aaronow ... they hold on to their money ...

Moss All of 'em. They, *hey*: it happens to us all.

Aaronow Where am I going to work?

Moss You have to cheer up, George, you aren't out yet.

Aaronow I'm not?

Moss You missed a fucking sale. Big deal. A deadbeat Polack. Big deal. How you going to sell 'em in the *first* place . . . ? Your mistake, you shoun'a took the lead.

Aaronow I had to.

Moss You had to, yeah. Why?

Aaronow To get on the . . .

Moss To get on the board. Yeah. How you goan a get on the board sell'n a Polack? And I'll tell you, I'll tell you what *else.* You listening? I'll tell you what else: don't ever try to sell an Indian.

Aaronow I'd never try to sell an Indian.

Moss You get those names come up, you ever get 'em, 'Patel'?

Aaronow *Mmm* . . .

Moss You ever get 'em?

Aaronow Well, I think I had one once.

Moss You did?

Aaronow I . . . I don't know.

Moss You had one you'd know it. *Patel.* They keep coming up. I don't know. They like to talk to salesmen. (*Pause.*) They're *lonely*, something. (*Pause.*) They like to feel *superior*, I don't know. Never bought a fucking thing. You're sitting down 'The Rio Rancho *this*, the blah blah blah,' 'The Mountain View,' 'Oh yes. My brother told me that . . . ' They got a grapevine. Fuckin' Indians, George. Not my cup of tea. Speaking of which I want to tell you something: (*Pause.*) I never got a cup of tea with them. You see them in the restaurants. A supercilious race. What is this *look* on their face all the time? I don't know. (*Pause.*) I don't know. Their broads all look like they just got fucked with a dead *cat*, I don't know. (*Pause.*) I don't know. I don't like it. Christ . . .

Aaronow What?

Moss The whole fuckin' thing ... The pressure's just too great. You're ab ... you're absolu ... they're too important. All of them. You go in the door. I ... 'I got to *close* this fucker, or I don't eat lunch.' 'Or I don't win the *Cadillac* ...' ... we fuckin' work too hard. You work too hard. We all, I remember when we were at Platt ... huh? Glen Ross Farms ... *didn't* we sell a bunch of that ...?

Aaronow They came in and they, you know ...

Moss Well, they fucked it up.

Aaronow They did.

Moss They killed the goose.

Aaronow They did.

Moss And now ...

Aaronow We're stuck with *this* ...

Moss We're stuck with *this* fucking shit ...

Aaronow ... *this* shit ...

Moss It's too ...

Aaronow It is.

Moss Eh?

Aaronow It's too ...

Moss You get a bad month, all of a ...

Aaronow You're on this ...

Moss All of, they got you on this 'board' ...

Aaronow I, I ... I ...

Moss Some *contest* board ...

Aaronow I ...

Moss It's not right.

Aaronow It's not.

Moss No.

Pause.

Aaronow And it's not right to the *customers*.

Moss I know it's not. I'll tell you, you got, you know, you got ... what did I learn as a kid on Western? Don't sell a guy one car. Sell him *five* cars over fifteen years.

Aaronow That's right?

Moss Eh ... ?

Aaronow That's right?

Moss Goddam right, that's right. Guys come on: 'Oh, the blah blah blah, *I* know what I'll do: I'll go in and rob everyone blind and go to Argentina cause nobody even *thought* of this before.'

Aaronow ... that's right ...

Moss Eh?

Aaronow No. That's absolutely right.

Moss And so they kill the goose, I, I, I'll ... and a fuckin' *man*, worked all his *life* has got to ...

Aaronow ... that's right ...

Moss Cower in his *boots*.

Aaronow (*simultaneously with 'boots'*) Shoes, boots, yes ...

Moss For some fuckin' 'Sell ten thousand and you win the steak knives ... '

Aaronow For some *sales* pro ...

Moss ... Sales promotion, 'you *lose*, then we fire your' ... No. It's *medieval* ... it's wrong. 'Or we're going to fire your ass.' It's wrong.

Aaronow Yes.

Moss Yes, it is. And you know who's responsible?

Aaronow Who?

Moss You know who it is. It's Mitch. And Murray. Cause it doesn't have to be this way.

Aaronow No.

Moss Look at Jerry Graff. He's *clean*, he's doing business for *himself*, he's got his, that *list* of his with the *nurses* . . . see? You see? That's *thinking*. Why take ten per cent? A ten per cent comm . . . why are we giving the rest away? What are we giving ninety per . . . for *nothing*. For some jerk sit in the office tell you 'Get out there and close.' 'Go win the Cadillac.' Graff. He goes out and *buys*. He pays top dollar for the . . . you see?

Aaronow Yes.

Moss That's *thinking*. Now, he's got the leads, he goes in business for *himself*. He's . . . that's what I . . . that's *thinking*! 'Who? Who's got a steady *job*, a couple bucks nobody's touched, who?'

Aaronow Nurses.

Moss So Graff buys a fucking list of nurses, one grand – if he paid two I'll eat my hat – four, five thousand nurses, and he's going *wild* . . .

Aaronow . . . he is?

Moss He's doing *very* well.

Aaronow I heard that they were running cold.

Moss The nurses?

Aaronow Yes.

Moss You hear a *lot* of things . . . He's doing very well. He's doing *very* well.

Aaronow With River Oaks?

Moss River Oaks, Brook Farms. *All* of that shit. Somebody told me, you know what he's clearing *himself*? Fourteen, fifteen grand a *week*.

Aaronow Himself?

Moss That's what I'm *saying*. Why? The *leads*. He's got the good leads . . . what are we, we're sitting in the shit here. Why? We have to go to *them* to *get* them. Huh. Ninety per cent our sale, we're *paying* to the *office* for the *leads*.

Aaronow The leads, the overhead, the telephones, there's *lots* of things.

Moss What do you need? A *telephone*, some broad to say 'Good morning,' nothing . . . nothing . . .

Aaronow No, it's not that simple, Dave . . .

Moss *Yes*. It *is*. It *is* simple, and you know what the hard part is?

Aaronow What?

Moss Starting up.

Aaronow What hard part?

Moss Of doing the thing. The dif . . . the difference. Between me and Jerry Graff. Going to business for yourself. The hard part is . . . you know what it is?

Aaronow What?

Moss Just the *act*.

Aaronow What act?

Moss To say 'I'm going on my own.' Cause what you do, George, let me tell you what you do: you find yourself in *thrall* to someone else. And we *enslave* ourselves. To *please*. To win some fucking *toaster* . . . to . . . to . . . and the guy who got there first made *up* those . . .

Aaronow . . . that's right . . .

Moss He made *up* those rules, and we're working for *him*.

Aaronow That's the truth . . .

Moss That's the *god's* truth. And it gets me depressed. I *swear* that it does. At MY AGE. To see a goddam: 'Somebody wins the Cadillac this month. P.S. Two guys get fucked.'

Aaronow *Huh*.

Moss You don't *axe* your sales force.

Aaronow No.

Moss You . . .

Aaronow You . . .

Moss You *build* it!

Aaronow That's what I . . .

Moss You fucking *build* it! Men come . . .

Aaronow Men come *work* for you . . .

Moss . . . you're absolutely right.

Aaronow They . . .

Moss They have . . .

Aaronow When they . . .

Moss Look look look look, when they *build* your business, then you can't fucking turn around, *enslave* them, treat them like *children*, fuck them up the ass, leave them to fend for themselves . . . no. (*Pause.*) No. (*Pause.*) You're absolutely right, and I want to tell you something.

Aaronow What?

Moss I want to tell you what somebody should do.

Aaronow What?

Moss Someone should stand up and strike *back*.

Aaronow What do you mean?

Moss *Somebody* . . .

Aaronow Yes . . . ?

Moss Should do something to *them*.

Aaronow What?

Moss Something. To pay them back.

Pause.

Someone, someone should hurt them. Murray and Mitch.

Aaronow Someone should hurt them.

Moss Yes.

Pause.

Aaronow How?

Moss How? Do something to hurt them. Where they live.

Aaronow What?

Pause.

Moss Someone should rob the office.

Aaronow Huh.

Moss That's what I'm *saying*. We were, if we were that kind of guys, to knock it off, and *trash* the joint, it looks like robbery, and *take* the fuckin' leads out of the files ... go to Jerry Graff.

Long pause.

Aaronow What could we get for them?

Moss What could we *get* for them? I don't know. Buck a *throw* ... buck-a-half a throw ... I don't know ... Hey, who knows what they're worth, what do they *pay* for them? All told ... must be, I'd ... three bucks a throw ... *I* don't know.

Aaronow How many leads have we got?

Moss The *Glengarry* ... the premium leads ...? I'd say we got five thousand. Five. Five thousand leads.

Aaronow And you're saying a fella could take and sell these leads to Jerry Graff.

Moss Yes.

Aaronow How do you know he'd buy them?

Moss Graff? Because I worked for him.

Aaronow You haven't talked to him.

Moss No. What do you mean? Have I talked to him about *this?*

Pause.

Aaronow Yes. I mean are you actually *talking* about this, or are we just . . .

Moss No, we're just . . .

Aaronow We're just '*talking*' about it.

Moss We're just *speaking* about it. (*Pause.*) As an *idea.*

Aaronow As an idea.

Moss Yes.

Aaronow We're not actually *talking* about it.

Moss No.

Aaronow Talking about it as a . . .

Moss *No.*

Aaronow As a *robbery.*

Moss As a 'robbery'?! No.

Aaronow *Well.* Well . . .

Moss *Hey.*

Pause.

Aaronow So all this, um, you didn't, actually, you didn't actually go talk to Graff.

Moss Not actually, no.

Pause.

Aaronow You didn't?

Moss No. Not actually.

Aaronow Did you?

Moss What did I say?

Aaronow What did you say?

Moss Yes. (*Pause.*) I said 'Not actually'. The fuck you care, George? We're just *talking* . . .

Aaronow We are?

Moss Yes.

Pause.

Aaronow Because, because, you know, it's a *crime*.

Moss That's right. It's a crime. It is a crime. It's also very safe.

Aaronow You're actually *talking* about this?

Moss That's right.

Pause.

Aaronow You're going to steal the leads?

Moss Have I said that?

Pause.

Aaronow Are you?

Pause.

Moss Did I say that?

Aaronow Did you talk to Graff?

Moss Is that what I said?

Aaronow What did he say?

Moss What did he say? He'd *buy* them.

Pause.

Aaronow You're going to steal the leads and sell the leads to him?

Pause.

Moss Yes.

Aaronow What will he pay?

Moss A buck a shot.

Aaronow For five thousand?

Moss However they are, that's the deal. A buck a throw. Five thousand dollars. Split it half and half.

Aaronow You're saying 'me'.

Moss Yes. (*Pause.*) Twenty-five hundred apiece. One night's work, and the job with Graff. Working the premium leads.

Pause.

Aaronow A job with Graff.

Moss Is that what I said?

Aaronow He'd give me a job.

Moss He would take you on. Yes.

Pause.

Aaronow Is that the truth?

Moss Yes. It is, George. (*Pause.*) Yes. It's a big decision. (*Pause.*) And it's a big reward. (*Pause.*) It's a big reward. For one night's work. (*Pause.*) But it's got to be tonight.

Aaronow What?

Moss What? What? The *leads*.

Aaronow You have to steal the leads tonight?

Moss That's *right*, the guys are moving them down-town. After the thirtieth. Murray and Mitch. After the contest.

Aaronow You're, you're saying so you have to go in there tonight and . . .

Moss *You* . . .

Aaronow I'm sorry?

Moss *You*.

Pause.

Aaronow Me?

Moss *You* have to go in. (*Pause.*) *You* have to get the leads.

Pause.

Aaronow I do?

Moss Yes.

Aaronow I . . .

Moss It's not something for nothing, George, I took you in on this, you have to go. That's your thing. I've made the deal with Graff. I can't go. I can't go in, I've spoken on this too much. I've got a big mouth. (*Pause.*) 'The fucking leads' et cetera, blah blah blah ' . . . the fucking tight ass company . . . '

Aaronow They'll know when you go over to Graff . . .

Moss What will they know? That I stole the leads? I *didn't* steal the leads, I'm going to the *movies* tonight with a friend, and then I'm going to the Como Inn. Why did I go to Graff? I got a better deal. *Period*. Let 'em prove something. They can't prove anything that's not the case.

Pause.

Aaronow *Dave.*

Moss Yes.

Aaronow You want me to break into the office tonight and steal the leads?

Moss Yes.

Pause.

Aaronow No.

Moss Oh, yes, George.

Aaronow What does that mean?

Moss Listen to this. I have an alibi, I'm going to the Como Inn, why? Why? The place gets robbed, they're going to come looking for *me*. Why? Because I probably did it. Are you going to turn me in? (*Pause.*) George? Are you going to turn me in?

Aaronow What if you don't get caught?

Moss They come to you, you going to turn me in?

Aaronow Why would they come to me?

Moss They're going to come to *everyone*.

Aaronow Why would I *do* it?

Moss You wouldn't, George, that's why I'm talking to you. Answer me. They come to you. You going to turn me in?

Aaronow No.

Moss Are you sure?

Aaronow Yes. I'm sure.

Moss Then listen to this: I have to get those leads tonight. That's something I have to do. If I'm not at the *movies* ... if I'm not eating over at the Inn ... If you don't do this, then *I* have to come in here ...

Aaronow ... you don't have to come in.

Moss ... and *rob* the place ...

Aaronow ... I thought that we were only talking ...

Moss ... they *take* me, then. They're going to ask me who were my accomplices.

Aaronow *Me?*

Moss Absolutely.

Aaronow That's ridiculous.

Moss Well, to the law, you're an accessory. Before the fact.

Aaronow I didn't ask to be.

Moss Then tough luck, George, because you are.

Aaronow Why? *Why*, because you only *told* me about it?

Moss That's right.

Aaronow Why are you doing this to me, Dave? Why are you talking this way to me? I don't understand. Why are you doing this at *all* ... ?

Moss That's none of your fucking business ...

Aaronow   Well, well, well, *talk* to me, we sat down to eat *dinner*, and here I'm a *criminal* . . .

Moss   You *went* for it.

Aaronow   In the abstract . . .

Moss   So I'm making it concrete.

Aaronow   Why?

Moss   Why? Why *you* going to give me five grand?

Aaronow   Do you need five grand?

Moss   Is that what I just said?

Aaronow   You need money? Is that the . . .

Moss   Hey, hey, let's just keep it simple, what I need is not the . . . what do *you* need . . . ?

Aaronow   What is the five grand? (*Pause.*) What is the, you said that we were going to *split* five . . .

Moss   I lied. (*Pause.*) Alright? My end is *my* business. Your end's twenty-five. In or out. You tell me, you're out you take the consequences.

Aaronow   I do?

Moss   Yes.

Pause.

Aaronow   And why is that?

Moss   Because you listened.

Scene Three

The restaurant. **Roma** *is seated alone at the booth.* **Lingk** *is at the booth next to him.* **Roma** *is talking to him.*

Roma   . . . all train compartments smell vaguely of shit. It gets so you don't mind it. That's the worst thing that I can confess. You know how long it took me to get there? A long time. When you *die* you're going to regret the things you don't do. You think you're *queer* . . . ? I'm going to tell you something: we're *all* queer. You think that you're a *thief*? So *what*? You get befuddled by a middle-class morality . . . ? Get *shut* of it. Shut it out. You cheated on your wife . . . ? You *did* it, *live* with it. (*Pause.*) You fuck little girls, so *be* it. There's an absolute morality? May *be*. And *then* what? If you *think* there is, then *be* that thing. Bad people go to hell? I don't *think* so. If you think that, act that way. A hell exists on earth? Yes. I won't live in it. That's *me*. You ever take a dump made you feel you'd just slept for twelve hours . . . ?

Lingk Did I . . . ?

Roma Yes.

Lingk I don't know.

Roma Or a *piss* . . . ? A great meal fades in reflection. Everything else gains. You know why? Cause it's only food. This shit we eat, it keeps us going. But it's only food. The great fucks that you may have had. What do you remember about them?

Lingk What do I . . . ?

Roma Yes.

Lingk Mmmm . . . ?

Roma I don't know. For *me*, I'm saying, what it is, it's probably not the orgasm. Some broads, forearms on your neck, something her *eyes* did. There was a *sound* she made . . . or, me, lying, in the, I'll tell you: me lying in bed: the next day she brought me *café au lait*. She gives me a cigarette, my balls feel like concrete. Eh? What I'm saying, What is our life: (*Pause.*) it's looking forward or it's looking back. And that's our life. That's *it*. Where is the *moment*? (*Pause.*) And what is it that we're afraid of? Loss. What else? (*Pause.*) The *bank* closes. We get *sick*, my wife died on a plane, the stock market collapsed . . . the house burnt down . . . what of these happen . . . ? None of 'em. We worry anyway. What does this mean? I'm not *secure*. How can I be secure? (*Pause.*) Through amassing wealth beyond all measure? No. And what's beyond all measure? That's a sickness. That's a trap. There is no measure. Only greed. How can we act? The right way, we would say, to deal with this: 'there is a one-in-a-million chance that so and so will happen ... *Fuck* it, it won't happen to *me*' ... No. We know that's not right, I think, we say the correct way to deal with this is 'There is a one in so-and-so chance this will happen ... God *protect* me. I am powerless, let it not happen to me ... ' But no to *that*. I say. There's something else. What is it? 'If it happens, AS IT MAY for that is not within our powers, I will *deal* with it, just as I do *today* with what draws my concern today.' I say *this* is how we must act. I do those things which seem correct to me *today*. I trust myself. And if security concerns me, I do that which *today* I think will make me secure. And every day I *do* that, when that day *arrives* that I need a reserve, a) odds are that I have it and, b) the *true* reserve that I have is the strength that I have of *acting each day* without fear. (*Pause.*) According to the dictates of my mind. (*Pause.*) Stocks, bonds, objects of art, real estate. Now: what are they? (*Pause.*) An opportunity. To what? To make money? Perhaps. To *lose* money? Perhaps. To 'indulge' and to 'learn' about ourselves? Perhaps. *So fucking what?* What *isn't?* They're an *opportunity*. That's all. They're an *event*. A guy comes up to you, you make a call, you send in a brochure, it doesn't matter, 'There these *properties* I'd like for you to see.' What does it mean? What you *want* it to mean. (*Pause.*) Money? (*Pause.*) If that's what it signifies to you. Security? (*Pause.*) Comfort? 'Some schmuck wants to make a buck on me'; or, 'I feel a vibration *fate* is calling' ... all it is is THINGS THAT HAPPEN TO YOU. (*Pause.*) That's all it is. How are they different? (*Pause.*) Some poor newly married guy gets run down by a cab. Some *busboy* wins the lottery ... (*Pause.*) All it is, it's a carnival. What's special ... what *draws* us ... ? (*Pause.*) We're all different. (*Pause.*) We're not the same ... (*Pause.*) We're not the same ... (*Pause.*) Hmmm ... (*Pause. Sighs.*) It's been a long day. (*Pause.*) What are you drinking?

Lingk Gimlet.

Roma Well, let's have a couple more. My name is Richard Roma, what's yours?

Lingk Lingk. James Lingk.

Roma James. I'm glad to meet you. (*They shake hands.*) I'm glad to meet you, James. (*Pause.*) I want to show you something. (*Pause.*) It might mean *nothing* to you ... and it might not. I don't know. I don't know anymore. (*Pause. He takes out a small map and spreads it on a table.*) What is that? Florida. Glengarry Highlands. Florida. 'Florida. *Bullshit.*' And maybe that's true; and that's what *I* said: but look *here*: What is this? This is a piece of land. Listen to what I'm going to tell you now:

Act Two

The Real Estate Office. Ransacked. A broken plate glass window boarded up, glass all over the floor. **Aaronow** *and* **Williamson** *standing around, smoking.*

Pause.

Aaronow People used to say that there are numbers of such magnitude that multiplying them by two made no difference.

Pause.

Williamson Who used to say that?

Aaronow In school.

Pause.

Baylen, *a detective, comes out of the inner office.*

Baylen Alright . . . ?

Roma *enters from the street.*

Roma *Williamson . . . Williamson*, they stole the *contracts* . . . ?

Baylen Excuse me, sir . . .

Roma Did they get my contracts?

Williamson They got . . .

Baylen Excuse me, fella.

Roma . . . did they . . .

Baylen Would you excuse us, please . . . ?

Roma Don't *fuck* with me, fella. I'm talking about a fuckin' Cadillac car that you owe me . . .

Williamson They didn't get your contract. I filed it before I left.

Roma They didn't get my contracts?

Williamson They: excuse me ... (*He goes back into the inner room with the detective.*)

Roma Oh, *fuck. Fuck.* (*He starts kicking the desk.*) FUCK FUCK FUCK! WILLIAMSON!!! WILLIAMSON!!! (*He goes to the door* **Williamson** *went into, tries the door, it's locked.*) OPEN THE FUCKING ... WILLIAMSON ...

Baylen (*coming out*) Who are you?

Williamson *comes out.*

Williamson They didn't get the contracts.

Roma Did they ...

Williamson They got, listen to me ...

Roma Th ...

Williamson Listen to me: they got *some* of them.

Roma Some of them ...

Baylen Who told you ...?

Roma Who told me wh ...? You've got a fuckin', you've ... a ... who is this ...? You've got a *board-up* on the window ... *Moss* told me.

Baylen (*looking back toward the inner office*) Moss ... Who told him?

Roma How the fuck do *I* know? (*To* **Williamson**.) *What* ... *talk* to me.

Williamson They took *some* of the con ...

Roma ... some of the contracts ... Lingk. James Lingk. I closed ...

Williamson You closed him yesterday.

Roma *Yes.*

Williamson It went down. I filed it.

Roma You did?

Williamson Yes.

Roma Then I'm over the fucking top and you owe me a Cadillac.

Williamson I . . .

Roma And I don't want any fucking shit and I don't give a shit, Lingk puts me over the top, you filed it, that's fine, any other shit kicks out *you* go back. You . . . *you* reclose it, cause I *closed* it and you . . . you owe me the car.

Baylen Would you excuse us, please.

Aaronow I, um, and may, maybe they're in, they're in . . . you should, John, if we're ins . . .

Williamson I'm sure that we're insured, George . . . (*Going back inside.*)

Roma Fuck insured. You owe me a car.

Baylen (*stepping back into his room*) Please don't leave. I'm going to talk to you. What's your name?

Roma Are you talking to me?

Pause.

Baylen Yes.

Pause.

Roma My name is Richard Roma.

Baylen *goes back into the inner room.*

Aaronow I, you know, they should be insured.

Roma What do *you* care . . . ?

Aaronow Then, you know, they wouldn't be so ups . . .

Roma Yeah. That's swell. Yes. You're right. (*Pause.*) How are you?

Aaronow I'm fine. You mean the *board*? You mean the *board* . . . ?

Roma I don't . . . yes. Okay, the board.

Aaronow I'm, I'm, I'm, I'm fucked on the board. *You*. You see how . . . I . . . (*Pause*.) I can't . . . my mind must be in other places. Cause I can't do any . . .

Roma *What*? You can't do *what*?

Pause.

Aaronow I can't close 'em.

Roma Well, they're old. I saw the shit they were giving you.

Aaronow Yes.

Roma Huh?

Aaronow Yes. They are old.

Roma They're ancient.

Aaronow Clear . . .

Roma Clear Meadows. That shit's dead.

Pause.

Aaronow It *is* dead.

Roma It's a waste of time.

Aaronow Yes. (*Long pause*.) I'm no fucking good.

Roma That's . . .

Aaronow Everything I . . . *you* know . . .

Roma That's not . . . Fuck that shit, George. You're a, *hey*, you had a bad month. You're a good man, George.

Aaronow I am?

Roma You hit a bad streak. We've all . . . look at this: fifteen units Mountain View, the fucking things get stole.

Aaronow He said he filed . . .

Roma He filed half of them, he filed the *big* one. All the little one, I have, I have to go back and . . . ah *fuck*, I got to go out like a fucking schmuck hat in my hand and reclose the . . .

(*Pause.*) I mean, talk about a fucking streak, that would sap *anyone's* self-confi ... I got to go out and reclose all my ... Where's the phones?

Aaronow They stole ...

Roma They stole the ...

Aaronow What. What kind of outfit are we running where ... where anyone ...

Roma (*to himself*) They stole the phones.

Aaronow Where *criminals* can come in here ... they take the ... They stole the phones.

Roma They stole the leads. They're ... *Christ.* (*Pause.*) What am I going to do this month? Oh *shit* ... (*He starts for the door.*)

Aaronow You think they're going to catch ... where are you going?

Roma Down the street.

Williamson *sticks his head out of the door.*

Williamson Where are you going?

Roma To the restaura ... what do you fucking ... ?

Williamson ... aren't you going out today?

Roma With what? (*Pause.*) With what, John, they took the leads ...

Williamson I have the stuff from last year's ...

Roma Oh. Oh. Oh your 'Nostalgia' file, that's fine. No. Swell. Cause I don't have to ...

Williamson ... you want to go out today ... ?

Roma Cause I don't have to *eat* this month. No. Okay. *Give* 'em to me ... (*To himself.*) Fucking Mitch and Murray going to shit a br ... what am I going to *do* all ...

Williamson *starts back into the office. He is accosted by* **Aaronow**.

Aaronow Were the leads . . .

Roma . . . what am I going to *do* all month . . . ?

Aaronow Were the leads insured?

Williamson (*long suffering*) I don't know, George, why?

Aaronow Cause, you know, cause they weren't, I know that Mitch and Murray uh . . .

Pause.

Williamson What?

Aaronow That they're going to be upset.

Williamson That's right. (*Going back into his office. To* **Roma**.) You want to go out today . . . ? (*Pause.*)

Aaronow He said we're all going to have to go talk to the guy.

Roma What?

Aaronow He said we . . .

Roma To the cop?

Aaronow Yeah.

Roma Yeah. That's swell. *Another* waste of time.

Aaronow A waste of time? Why?

Roma *Why?* Cause they aren't going to find the guy.

Aaronow The cops?

Roma Yes. The cops. No.

Aaronow They aren't?

Roma No.

Aaronow Why don't you think so?

Roma Why? Because they're *stupid*. 'Where were you last night . . . ?'

Aaronow Where were you?

Roma Where was *I*?

Aaronow Yes.

Roma I was at home, where were *you*?

Aaronow At home.

Roma *See* . . . ? Were you the guy who broke in?

Aaronow Was I?

Roma Yes.

Aaronow No.

Roma Then don't sweat it, George, you know why?

Aaronow No.

Roma You have nothing to hide.

Aaronow (*pause*) When I talk to the police, I get nervous.

Roma Yeah. You know who doesn't?

Aaronow No, who?

Roma Thieves.

Aaronow Why?

Roma They're inured to it.

Aaronow You think so?

Roma Yes.

Pause.

Aaronow But what should I *tell* them?

Roma The truth, George. Always tell the truth. It's the easiest thing to remember.

Williamson *comes out of the office with leads*. **Roma** *takes one, reads it.*

Roma *Patel*? Ravidam *Patel*? How am I going to make a living on these deadbeat *wogs*? Where did you get this, from the *morgue*?

Williamson If you don't want it, give it back.

Roma I don't 'want' it, if you catch my drift.

Williamson I'm giving you *three* leads. You . . .

Roma What's the fucking point in *any* case . . . ? What's the *point?* I got to argue with *you*, I got to knock heads with the *cops*, I'm busting my *balls*, sell your *dirt* to fucking *deadbeats* money in the *mattress*, I come back you can't even manage to keep the contracts safe, I have to go back and close them *again* . . . what the fuck am I wasting my time, fuck this shit. I'm going out and reclose last week's stuff . . .

Williamson Don't do it, they might find him.

Roma They might find the guy?

Williamson Yes.

Roma Your 'source' tells you that?

Williamson The word from Murray is: leave them alone. If we have to get a new sig he'll go out himself, he'll be the *President*, just come *in*, from out of *town* . . .

Roma Okay, okay, okay, gimme this shit. Fine. (*He takes the leads.*)

Williamson I'm giving you three . . .

Roma Three? I count *two*.

Williamson Three.

Roma Patel? Fuck *you*. Fuckin' *Shiva* handed him a million dollars, told him 'sign the deal', he wouldn't sign. And Vishnu, too. Into the bargain. Fuck *that*, John. You know your business, I know mine. Your business is being an *asshole*, and I find out whose fucking *cousin* you are, I'm going to go to him and figure out a way to have your *ass* . . . fuck you – I'll wait for the new leads.

Levene *enters.*

Levene Get the *chalk*. Get the *chalk* . . . get the *chalk*! I closed 'em! I *closed* the cocksucker. Get the chalk and put me on the *board*. I'm going to Hawaii! Put me on the Cadillac board, Williamson! Pick up the fuckin' chalk. Eight units. Mountain View . . .

Roma You sold eight Mountain View?

Levene You bet your ass. Who wants to go to lunch? Who wants to go to lunch? I'm buying. (*He slaps a contract down on* **Williamson**'s *desk*.) Eighty-two fucking grand. And twelve grand in commission. John. (*Pause*.) On fucking deadbeat magazine subscription leads.

Williamson Who?

Levene (*pointing to the contract*) *Read* it. Bruce and Harriett Nyborg. (*Looking around*.) What happened here?

Aaronow Fuck. I had them on River Glen.

Levene *looks around*.

Levene What happened?

Williamson Somebody broke in.

Roma Eight units?

Levene That's right.

Roma *Shelly* . . . !

Levene Hey, big fucking deal. Broke a bad streak . . .

Aaronow Shelly, the Machine, Levene.

Levene You . . .

Aaronow That's great.

Levene Thank you, George.

Baylen *sticks his head out of the room, calls in 'Aaronow'*. **Aaronow** *goes into the side room*.

Levene Get on the phone, call Mitch . . .

Roma They took the phones . . .

Levene They . . .

Baylen *Aaronow* . . .

Roma They took the typewriters, they took the leads, they took the *cash*, they took the *contracts* . . .

Levene Wh . . . wh . . . Wha . . . ?

Aaronow We had a robbery.

Pause.

Levene When?

Roma Last night, this morning...

Pause.

Levene They took the leads?

Roma Mmm.

Moss *comes out of the interrogation.*

Moss Fuckin' asshole.

Roma What, they beat you with a rubber bat?

Moss Cop couldn't find his dick two hands and a map. Anyone talks to this guy's an *asshole*...

Roma You going to turn States?

Moss Fuck you, Ricky. I ain't going out today. I'm going home. I'm going home because nothing's *accomplished* here ...Anyone *talks* to this guy is...

Roma Guess what the Machine did?

Moss Fuck the Machine.

Roma Mountain View. Eight units.

Moss Fuckin' cop's got no right talk to me that way. I didn't rob the place...

Roma You hear what I said?

Moss Yeah. He closed a deal.

Roma Eight units. Mountain View.

Moss (*to* **Levene**) You did that?

Levene Yeah.

Pause.

Moss Fuck you.

Roma Guess who?

Moss When...

Levene Just now.

Roma Guess who?

Moss You just this morning...

Roma Harriett and blah blah Nyborg.

Moss You did that?

Levene Eighty-two thousand dollars.

Pause.

Moss Those fuckin' *deadbeats*...

Levene My ass. I told 'em. (*To* **Roma**.) Listen to this: I said...

Moss Hey, I don't want to hear your fucking war stories...

Roma Fuck *you*, Dave...

Levene 'You have to believe in your*self*... you,' look, 'alright...?'

Moss (*to* **Williamson**) Give me some leads. I'm going out ... I'm getting out of...

Levene '... you have to believe in your*self*...'

Moss Na, fuck the leads, I'm going home.

Levene 'Bruce, Harriett... Fuck *me*, believe in your*self*...'

Roma ... we haven't got a lead...

Moss Why not?

Roma They took 'em...

Moss Hey, they're fuckin' garbage any case... This whole goddam...

Levene '... You look around, you say "this one has so-and-so, and I have nothing"...'

Moss *Shit*.

Levene '*Why*? Why don't I get the opportunities...?'

Moss And did they steal the contracts ... ?

Roma Fuck *you* care ... ?

Levene 'I want to tell you something, Harriett ... '

Moss ... the fuck is *that* supposed to mean ... ?

Levene Will you shut up, I'm telling you this ...

Aaronow *sticks his head out.*

Aaronow Can we get some coffee ... ?

Moss How ya doing?

Pause.

Aaronow Fine.

Moss Uh huh.

Aaronow If anyone's going, I could use some coffee.

Levene 'You *do* get the ... ' (*To* **Roma**.) Huh? Huh?

Moss *Fuck* is that supposed to mean?

Levene 'You *do* get the opportunity ... You *get* them. As *I* do, as *anyone* does ... '

Moss Ricky? ... That I don't care they stole the contracts? (*Pause.*)

Levene I got 'em in the kitchen. I'm eating her crumb cake.

Moss What does that mean?

Roma It *means*, Dave, you haven't closed a good one in a month, none of my business, you want to push me to answer you. (*Pause.*) And so you haven't got a contract to get stolen or so forth.

Moss You have a mean streak in you, Ricky, you know that ...

Levene Rick. Let me tell you. Wait, we're in the ...

Moss Shut the fuck up. (*Pause.*) Ricky. You have a mean streak in you ... (*To* **Levene**.) And what the fuck are *you* babbling about ... ? (*To* **Roma**.) Bring that shit up. Of my

volume. You were on a bad one and I brought it up to *you*
you'd harbor it. (*Pause.*) You'd harbor it a long long while.
And you'd be right.

Roma Who said 'Fuck the Machine'?

Moss '*Fuck the Machine*'? '*Fuck the Machine*'? What is this?
Courtesy class . . . ? You're *fucked*, Rick – are you fucking *nuts*?
You're hot, so you think you're the *ruler* of this place . . . ?!
You want to . . .

Levene Dave . . .

Moss . . . Shut up. Decide who should be dealt with how? Is
that the thing? I come into the fuckin' office today, I get
humiliated by some jagoff cop. I get accused of . . . I get this
shit thrown in my face by you, you genuine shit, because
you're top name on the board . . .

Roma Is that what I did? Dave? I humiliated you? My *God*
. . . I'm *sorry* . . .

Moss Sittin' on top of the *world*, sittin' on top of the *world*,
everything's fucking *peach*fuzz . . .

Roma Oh, and I don't get a moment to spare for a bust-out
humanitarian down on his luck lately. Fuck *you*, Dave, you
know you got a big *mouth*, and *you* make a close the whole *place*
stinks with your *farts* for a week. 'How much you just
ingested,' what a big *man* you are, 'Hey, let me buy you a
pack of gum. I'll show you how to *chew* it.' Your *pal* closes, all
that comes out of your mouth is *bile*, how fucked *up* you
are . . .

Moss *Who's* my pal . . . ? And what are you, Ricky, huh,
what are you, Bishop *Sheean*? Who the fuck are *you*, Mr Slick
. . . ? What are you, friend to the *workingman*? Big deal. Fuck
you, you got the memory a fuckin' *fly*. I never liked you.

Roma What is this, your farewell speech?

Moss I'm going home.

Roma Your farewell to the troops?

Moss I'm not going home. I'm going to Wis*con*sin.

Roma Have a good trip.

Moss Fuck you. Fuck the *lot* of you. Fuck you *all*.

Moss *exits. Pause.*

Roma (*to* **Levene**) You were saying? (*Pause.*) Come on. Come on, you got them in the kitchen, you got the stats spread out, you're in your shirtsleeves, you can *smell* it. Huh? Snap out of it, you're eating her *crumb* cake.

Pause.

Levene I'm eating her *crumb* cake . . .

Roma . . . how was it . . . ?

Levene From the store.

Roma . . . fuck *her* . . .

Levene 'What we have to do is *admit* to ourself that we see that opportunity . . . and *take* it. (*Pause.*) And that's it.' And we *sit* there . . . (*Pause.*) I got the pen out . . .

Roma Always Be Closing . . .

Levene That's what I'm *saying*. The *old* ways. The *old* ways . . . convert the mother fucker . . . *sell* him . . . *sell* him . . . *make him sign the check*. (*Pause.*) The . . . Bruce, Harriett . . . the kitchen, blah: They got their money in *government* bonds . . . I say *fuck* it, we're going to go the whole route. I plat it out eight units. Eighty-two grand. I tell them. 'This is now. This is that *thing* that you've been dreaming of, you're going to find that suitcase on the train, the guy comes in the door, the bag that's full of money. This is it, *Harriett* . . .'

Roma (*reflectively*) Harriett . . .

Levene Bruce . . . 'I don't want to fuck *around* with you. I don't want to go *round* this, and *pussyfoot* around the thing, you have to look back on this. I do, too. I came here to do good for you and me. For *both* of us. Why take an interim position? *The only arrangement I'll accept* is full investment. Period. The whole eight units. I know that you're saying 'be safe', I know what you're saying. I know if I left you to yourselves, you'd say 'come back tomorrow' and when I walked out that door, you'd make a cup of *coffee* . . . you'd sit *down* . . . and you'd think 'let's be safe . . . ' and not to disappoint me you'd go *one* unit or maybe two, because you'd become scared because you'd met possi*bil*ity. But this won't do, and that's not the subject . . . ' Listen to this, I actually said this: 'That's not the subject of our *evening* together.' Now I handed them the pen. I held it in my hand. I turned the contract eight units eighty-two grand. 'Now I want you to sign.' (*Pause.*) I sat there. Five minutes. Then, I sat there, Ricky, *twenty-two minutes* by the kitchen *clock*. (*Pause.*) Twenty-two minutes by the kitchen clock. Not a *word*, not a *motion*. What am I thinking? 'My arm's getting tired'? *No.* I *did* it. Like in the *old* days, Ricky. Like I was taught . . . Like, like, like I *used* to do . . . I did it.

Roma Like you taught me . . .

Levene Bullshit, you're . . . No. That's raw . . . well, if I *did*, them I'm *glad* I did. I, *well*. I locked on them. All on them, nothing on me. All my thoughts are on them. I'm holding the last thought that I spoke: 'Now is the time.' (*Pause.*) They signed, Ricky. It was *great*. It was fucking great. It was like they wilted all at once. No *gesture* . . . nothing. Like together. They, I swear to God, they both kind of *imperceptibly slumped*. And he reaches and takes the pen and signs, he passes it to her, she signs. It was so fucking solemn. I just let it sit. I nod like this. I nod again. I grasp his hands. I shake his hands. I grasp *her* hands. I nod at her like this. 'Bruce . . . Harriett . . . ' I'm beaming at them. I'm nodding like this. I point back in the living-room, back to the sideboard. (*Pause.*) *I didn't fucking know there was a sideboard there*!! He goes back, he brings us a drink. Little shotglasses. A pattern in 'em. And we toast. In silence.

Pause.

Roma That was a great sale, Shelly.

Pause.

Levene . . . Ah fuck.

Williamson *sticks his head out of the office.*

Levene Leads! Leads! Williamson! Send me *out*! Send me *out*!

Williamson The leads are coming.

Levene *Get* 'em to me!

Williamson I talked to Murray and Mitch an hour ago. They're coming in, you understand they're a bit *upset* over this morning's . . .

Levene Did you tell 'em my sale?

Williamson How could I tell 'em your sale? Eh? I don't have a tel . . . I'll tell 'em your sale when they bring in the leads. Alright? Shelly. Alright? We had a little . . . You closed a deal. You made a good sale. Fine.

Levene It's better than a good sale. It's a . . .

Williamson Look: I have a lot of things on my mind, they're coming in, alright, they're very upset, I'm trying to make some *sense* . . .

Levene All that I'm *telling* you: that one thing you can tell them it's a remarkable sale.

Williamson The only thing remarkable is who you made it to.

Levene What does *that* fucking mean?

Williamson That if the sale sticks, it will be a miracle.

Levene Why should the sale not stick? Hey, fuck *you*. That's what I'm saying. You have no idea of your job. A man's his job and you're *fucked* at yours. You hear what I'm saying to you? Your 'end of month board' . . . You can't run an office. I don't care. You don't know what it *is*, you don't have the *sense*, you don't have the *balls*. You ever been on a sit? *Ever*? Has this cocksucker ever been . . . you ever sit down with a cust . . .

Williamson I were you, I'd calm down, Shelly.

Levene *Would* you? *Would* you . . . ? Or you're gonna *what*, fire me?

Williamson It's not impossible.

Levene On an eighty-thousand dollar *day*? And it ain't even *noon*.

Roma You closed 'em today?

Levene Yes. I did. This *morning*. (*To* **Williamson**.) What I'm *saying* to you: things can *change*. You *see*? This is where you fuck *up*, because this is something you don't *know*. You can't look down the *road*. And see what's *coming*. Might be someone *else*, John. It might be someone *new*, eh? Someone *new*. And you can't look *back*. Cause you don't know *history*. You ask them. When we were at Rio Rancho, who was top man? A month . . . ? Two months . . . ? Eight months in twelve for three years in a row. You know what that means? You know what that means? Is that *luck*? Is that some, some, some purloined leads? That's *skill*. That's *talent*, that's, that's . . .

Roma . . . *yes* . . .

Levene . . . and you don't *remember*. Cause you weren't *around*. That's cold *calling*. Walk up to the door. I don't even know their *name*. I'm selling something they don't even *want*. You talk about soft sell . . . before we had a name for it . . . before we called it anything, we did it.

Roma That's right, Shel.

Levene And, and, and, I *did* it. And I put a kid through *school*. She . . . and . . . Cold *calling* fella. Door to door. But you don't know. You don't know. You never heard of a *streak*. You ever heard of 'marshalling your sales force' . . . what are you, you're a *secretary*, John. Fuck *you*. That's my message to you. Fuck you and kiss my ass. You don't like it, I'll go talk to Jerry Graff. Period. Fuck you. Put me on the board. And I want three worthwhile leads today and I don't want any bullshit about them and I want 'em close together cause I'm going to hit them all today. That's all I have to say to you.

Roma He's right, Williamson.

Williamson *goes into a side office. Pause.*

Levene It's not right. I'm sorry, and I'll tell you who's to blame is Mitch and Murray.

Roma *sees something outside the window.*

Roma (*sotto*) Oh Christ.

Levene The hell with him. We'll go to lunch, the leads won't be up for . . .

Roma You're a client. I just sold you five waterfront Glengarry Farms. I rub my head, throw me the cue 'Kenilworth'.

Levene . . . What is it?

Roma Kenilw . . .

James Lingk *enters the office.*

Roma (*to* **Levene**) *I* own the property, my *mother* owns the property, I put her *into* it. I'm going to show you on the plats. You look when you get home A–3 through A–14 and 26 through 30. You take your time and if you still feel.

Levene No, Mr Roma. I don't need the time, I've made a lot of *investments* in the last . . .

Lingk I've got to talk to you.

Roma (*looking up*) Jim! What are you doing here? Jim Lingk, D. Ray Morton . . .

Levene Glad to meet you.

Roma I just put Jim into Black Creek . . . are you acquainted with . . .

Levene No . . . Black *Creek*. Yes. In *Florida*?

Roma Yes.

Levene I wanted to *speak* with you about . . .

Roma Well, we'll do that this weekend.

Levene My *wife* told me to look into . . .

Roma *Beautiful*. Beautiful rolling land. I was telling Jim and Jinny, Ray, I want to tell you something. (*To* **Levene**.) You, Ray, you eat in a lot of restaurants. I know you do . . . (*To* **Lingk**.) Mr Morton's with American Express . . . he's (*To* **Levene**.) I can tell Jim what you do . . .

Levene Sure.

Roma Ray is Director of all European Sales and Services for American Ex . . . (*To* **Levene**.) But I'm saying you haven't had a *meal* until you've tasted . . . I was at the Lingks' last . . . as a matter of fact, what was that Service Feature you were talking about . . .

Levene Which . . .

Roma 'Home Cooking' . . . what did you call it, you said it . . . it was a tag phrase that you had . . .

Levene Uh . . .

Roma Home . . .

Levene Home cooking . . .

Roma The monthly interview . . . ?

Levene Oh! For the *magazine* . . .

Roma Yes. Is this something that I can talk ab . . .

Levene Well, it isn't coming *out* until the February iss . . . *sure*. Sure, go ahead, Rick.

Roma You're sure?

Levene (*nods*) Go ahead.

Roma Well, Ray was eating at one of his company's men's home in France . . . the man's French, isn't he?

Levene No, his *wife* is.

Roma Ah. Ah, his wife is. Ray: what *time* do you have . . . ?

Levene Twelve fifteen.

Roma Oh! My God . . . I've got to get you on the *plane*!

Levene Didn't I say I was taking the two o' . . .

Roma No. You said the One. That's why you said we couldn't talk till Kenilworth.

Levene Oh, my God, you're right! I'm on the One . . . (*Getting up.*) Well, let's *scoot* . . .

Lingk I've got to talk to you . . .

Roma I've got to get Ray to O'Hare . . . (*To* **Levene**.) Come on, let's hustle . . . (*Over his shoulder.*) John! Call American Express in *Pittsburgh* for Mr Morton, will you, tell them he's on the one o'clock. (*To* **Lingk**.) I'll see you . . . Christ, I'm sorry you came all the way in . . . I'm running Ray over to O'Hare . . . You wait here, I'll . . . no. (*To* **Levene**.) I'm meeting your man at the Bank . . . (*To* **Lingk**.) I wish you'd phoned . . . I'll tell you, wait: (*To* **Lingk**.) Are you and Jinny going to be home tonight? (*He rubs his forehead.*)

Lingk I . . .

Levene Rick.

Roma What?

Levene *Kenilworth* . . . ?

Roma I'm sorry . . . ?

Levene *Kenilworth.*

Roma Oh, God . . . Oh, God . . . (**Roma** *takes* **Lingk** *aside, sotto.*) Jim, excuse me . . . Ray, I told you, who he is is *the* Senior Vice-President American Express. His family owns thirty-two per . . . Over the past years I've sold him . . . I can't tell you the dollar amount, but *quite* a lot of land. I promised five *weeks* ago that I'd go to the wife's birthday party in Kenilworth tonight. (*He sighs.*) I *have* to go. You understand. They treat me like a member of the family, so I have to go. It's funny, you know, you get a picture of the Corporation Type Company Man, all business . . . this man, *no*. We'll go out to his home sometime. Let's see. (*He checks his datebook.*) Tomorrow. No. Tomorrow, I'm in L.A. . . . *Monday* . . . I'll take you to lunch, where would you like to go?

Lingk My wife . . .

Roma *rubs his head.*

Levene (*standing in the door*) Rick . . . ?

Roma I'm sorry, Jim. I can't talk now. I'll call you tonight
. . . I'm sorry. I'm coming, Ray.

He starts for the door.

Lingk My wife said I have to cancel the deal.

Roma It's a common reaction, Jim. I'll tell you what it is,
and I know that that's why you married her. One of the
reasons is *prudence*. It's a sizeable investment. One thinks *twice*
. . . it's also something *women* have. It's just a reaction to the
size of the investment. *Monday*, if you'd invite me for dinner
again . . . (*To* **Levene**.) This woman can *cook* . . .

Levene (*simultaneously*) I'm sure she can . . .

Roma (*to* **Lingk**) We're going to talk. I'm going to *tell* you
something. Because (*Sotto.*) there's something about your
acreage I want you to know. I can't talk about it now. I
really shouldn't. And, in fact, by *law*, I . . . (*He shrugs,
resigned.*) The man next to you, he bought his lot at forty-*two*,
he phoned to say that he'd *already* had an offer . . . (**Roma**
rubs his head.)

Levene Rick . . . ?

Roma I'm coming, Ray . . . what a day! I'll call you this
evening, Jim. I'm sorry you had to come in . . . Monday,
lunch.

Lingk My wife . . .

Levene Rick, we really have to go.

Lingk My wife . . .

Roma Monday.

Lingk She called the Consumer . . . the Attorney, I don't
know. The Attorney Gen . . . they said we have three days . . .

Roma *Who* did she call?

Lingk I don't know, the Attorney Gen . . . the . . . some Consumer office, umm . . .

Roma Why did she do *that*, Jim?

Lingk I don't know. (*Pause.*) They said we have three days. (*Pause.*) They said we have three days.

Roma Three days.

Lingk To . . . you know. (*Pause.*)

Roma No I don't know. *Tell* me.

Lingk To change our minds.

Roma Of *course* you have three days.

Pause.

Lingk So we can't talk *Monday*.

Pause.

Roma Jim, Jim, you saw my book . . . I *can't, you* saw my book . . .

Lingk But we have to *before* Monday. To get our money ba . . .

Roma Three *business* days. They mean three *business* days.

Lingk Wednesday, Thursday, Friday.

Roma I don't understand.

Lingk That's what they are. Three business . . . if I wait till Monday, my time limit runs out.

Roma You don't count Saturday.

Lingk I'm not.

Roma No, I'm saying you don't include Saturday . . . in your three days. It's not a *business* day.

Lingk But I'm not *counting* it. (*Pause.*) Wednesday. Thursday. Friday. So it would have elapsed.

Roma What would have elapsed?

Lingk If we wait till Mon . . .

Roma When did you write the check?

Lingk Yest...

Roma What was yesterday?

Lingk Tuesday.

Roma And when was that check cashed?

Lingk I don't know.

Roma What was the *earliest* it could have been cashed?

Pause.

Lingk I don't know.

Roma *Today*. (*Pause*.) *Today*. Which, in any case, it was not, as there were a couple of points on the agreement I wanted to go over with you in any case.

Lingk The check wasn't cashed?

Roma I just called down-town, and it's on their desk.

Levene Rick...

Roma One moment, I'll be right with you. (*To* **Lingk**.) In fact, a ... *one* point, which I spoke to you of which (*He looks around*.) I can't talk to you about here.

Baylen *puts his head out of the doorway*.

Baylen Levene!!!

Lingk I, I ...

Roma Listen to me, the *statute*, it's for your protection. I have no complaints with that, in fact, I was a member of the board when we *drafted* it, so quite the *opposite*. It *says* that you can change your mind three working days from the time the deal is closed.

Baylen Levene!

Roma Which, wait a second, which is not until the check is cashed.

Baylen Levene!!

Aaronow *comes out of the* **Detective**'s *office.*

Aaronow I'm *through*, with *this* fucking mishagas. No one should talk to a man that way. How are you *talking* to me that . . . ?

Baylen Levene!

Williamson *puts his head out of the office.*

Aaronow . . . how can you *talk* to me that . . . that . . .

Levene (*to* **Roma**) Rick, I'm going to flag a cab.

Aaronow *I* didn't rob . . .

Williamson *sees* **Levene**.

Williamson Shelly: get in the office.

Aaronow *I* didn't . . . why should *I* . . . 'Where were you last . . . ' is anybody listening to me . . . ? Where's Moss . . . ? Where . . . ?

Baylen Levene! (*To* **Williamson**.) Is this Lev . . . (**Baylen** *accosting* **Lingk**.)

Levene (*taking* **Baylen** *into the office*) Ah. Ah. Perhaps I can advise you on that . . . (*To* **Roma** *and* **Lingk**, *as he exits.*) *Excuse* us, will you . . . ?

Aaronow (*simultaneous with* **Levene**'s *speech above*) . . . Come in here . . . I *work* here, I don't come in here to be *mistreated* . . .

Williamson Go to *lunch*, will you . . .

Aaronow I want to *work* today, that's why I came . . .

Williamson The leads come in, I'll let . . .

Aaronow . . . that's why I came in. I thought I . . .

Williamson Just go to lunch.

Aaronow I don't *want* to go to lunch.

Williamson Go to lunch, George.

Aaronow Where does he get off to talk that way to a working man? It's not . . .

Williamson (*buttonholes him*) Will you take it outside, *we* have people trying to do *business* here . . .

Aaronow That's what, that's what, that's what *I* was trying to do. (*Pause.*) That's why I came *in* . . . I meet *Gestapo* tac . . .

Williamson (*going back into his office*) Excuse me . . .

Aaronow I meet *Gestapo* tactics . . . I meet *Gestapo* tactics . . . that's not right . . . No man has the right to . . . 'call an attorney', that means you're guilt . . . you're under sus . . . 'Co', he says, 'Cooperate' or we'll go down-town. *That's* not . . . as long as I've . . .

Williamson (*bursting out of his office*) Will you get out of here? Will you get *out* of here? Will you? I'm trying to run an *office* here. Will you go to lunch? Go to lunch. Will you go to lunch? (*He retreats into his office.*)

Roma (*to* **Aaronow**) Will you excuse . . .

Aaronow Where did Moss . . . ? I . . .

Roma Will you excuse us please?

Aaronow Uh uh, did he go to the restaurant?

(*Pause.*) I . . . I . . . (*He exits.*)

Roma I'm *very* sorry, Jimmy. I apologize to you.

Lingk It's not me, it's my wife.

Roma (*pause*) What is?

Lingk I told you.

Roma Tell me again.

Lingk What's going on here?

Roma Tell me again. Your wife.

Lingk I told you.

Roma You tell me again.

Lingk She wants her money back.

Roma We're going to speak to her.

Lingk No. She told me 'right now'.

Roma We'll speak to her, Jim . . .

Lingk She won't listen.

Baylen *sticks his head out.*

Baylen *Roma.*

Lingk She told me if not, I have to call the State's Attorney.

Roma No, no. That's just something she 'said'. We don't have to do that.

Lingk She told me I *have* to.

Roma No, Jim.

Lingk I *do*. If I don't get my *money* back . . .

Williamson *points out* **Roma** *to him.*

Baylen Roma! (*To* **Roma**.) I'm talking to you . . .

Roma I've . . . look. (*Generally*.) Will someone get this guy off my back.

Baylen You have a problem?

Roma Yes, I have a problem. Yes, I *do*, my fr . . . It's not me that ripped the joint off, I'm doing *business*. I'll be with you in a *while*. You got it . . . ? (*He looks back,* **Lingk** *is heading for the door*.) Where are you going?

Lingk I'm . . .

Roma Where are you going . . . ? This is *me* . . . This is Ricky, Jim. Jim, anything you *want*, you *want* it, you *have* it. You understand? This is *me*. Something *upset* you. Sit down, now sit down. You tell me what it is. (*Pause*.) Am I going to help you fix it? You're goddamned right I am. Sit down. Tell you something . . . ? *Sometimes* we need someone from *outside*. It's . . . no, sit down . . . Now *talk* to me.

Lingk I can't negotiate.

Roma What does that mean?

Lingk That . . .

Roma ... what, what, *say* it. Say it to me ...

Lingk I ...

Roma What ... ?

Lingk I ...

Roma What ... ? Say the words.

Lingk I don't have the *power*. (*Pause.*) I said it.

Roma What power?

Lingk The power to negotiate.

Roma To negotiate what? (*Pause.*) To negotiate what?

Lingk *This.*

Roma What, 'this'?

Pause.

Lingk The deal.

Roma The 'deal', *forget* the deal. *Forget* the deal, you've got something on your mind, Jim, what is it?

Lingk (*rising*) I can't talk to you, *you* met my wife, I ...

Pause.

Roma What? (*Pause.*) What? (*Pause.*) What, Jim: I tell you what, let's get out of here ... let's go get a drink.

Lingk She told me not to talk to you.

Roma Let's ... no one's going to know, let's go around the *corner* and we'll get a drink.

Lingk She told me I had to get back the check or call the State's Att ...

Roma *Forget* the deal, Jimmy. (*Pause.*) *Forget* the deal ... you know me. The deal's *dead*. Am I talking about the *deal*? That's *over*. Please. Let's talk about *you*. Come on. (*Pause.* **Roma** *rises and starts walking toward the front door.*) Come on. (*Pause.*) Come on, Jim. (*Pause.*) I want to tell you something. Your life is your own. You have a contract with your wife. You have certain things you do *jointly*, you have a *bond* there

... and there are *other* things. Those things are yours. You needn't feel *ashamed*, you needn't feel that you're being *untrue* ... or that she would abandon you if she knew, this is your life. (*Pause.*) *Yes.* Now I want to *talk* to you because you're obviously upset and that *concerns* me. Now let's go. Right now.

Lingk *gets up and they start for the door.*

Baylen (*sticks his head out of the door*) Roma ...

Lingk ... and ... and ...

Pause.

Roma What?

Lingk And the check is ...

Roma What did I *tell* you? (*Pause.*) What did I say about the three days ... ?

Baylen Roma, would you, I'd like to get some lunch ...

Roma I'm talking with Mr Lingk. If you please, I'll be back in. (*He checks his watch.*) I'll be back in a while ... I told you, check with Mr Williamson.

Baylen The people down-town said ...

Roma You call them again. Mr Williamson ... !

Williamson Yes.

Roma Mr Lingk and I are going to ...

Williamson Yes. Please. Please. (*To* **Lingk**.) The police (*He shrugs.*) can be ...

Lingk What are the police doing?

Roma It's nothing ...

Lingk What are the *police* doing here ... ?

Williamson We had a slight burglary last night.

Roma It was nothing ... I was telling Mr Lingk ...

Williamson Mr Lingk. James Lingk. Your contract went out. Nothing to ...

Roma John . . .

Williamson Your contract went out to the bank.

Pause.

Lingk You cashed the check?

Williamson We . . .

Roma . . . Mr Williamson . . .

Williamson Your check was cashed yesterday afternoon.
And we're completely insured, as you know, in *any* case.
(*Pause.*)

Lingk (*to* **Roma**) You cashed the check?

Roma Not to my knowledge, no . . .

Williamson I'm sure we can . . .

Lingk Oh, Christ . . . (*He starts out the door.*) Don't follow me
. . . Oh, Christ . . . (*Pause. To* **Roma**.) I know I've let you
down. I'm sorry. For . . . Forgive . . . for . . . I don't know
anymore. (*Pause.*) Forgive me. (**Lingk** *exits.*) (*Pause.*)

Roma (*to* **Williamson**) You stupid fucking cunt. *You*,
Williamson . . . I'm talking to *you*, shithead . . . You just cost
me *six thousand dollars*. (*Pause.*) Six thousand dollars. And one
Cadillac. That's right. What are you going to do about it?
What are you going to do about it, asshole. You fucking *shit*.
Where did you learn your *trade*. You stupid fucking *cunt*. You
idiot. Whoever told you you could work with *men*?

Baylen Could I . . .

Roma I'm going to have your *job*, shithead. I'm going *down-
town* and talk to Mitch and Murray, and I'm going to
Lemkin. I don't care *whose* nephew you are, who you know,
whose dick you're sucking on. You're going *out*, I swear to
you, you're going . . .

n Hey, fella, let's get this done . . .

Anyone in this office lives on their *wits* . . . (*To
.*) I'm going to be with you in a second. (*To
nson.) What you're hired for is to *help* us – does that

seem clear to you? To *help* us. *Not* to fuck us up ... to help *men*
who are going *out* there to try to earn a *living*. You *fairy*. You
company man ... I'll tell you something else. I hope you
knocked the joint off, I can tell our friend here something
might help him to catch you. (*He starts into the room.*) You
want to learn the first rule you'd know if you ever spent a day
in life, you never open your mouth till you know what the
shot is. (*Pause.*) You fuckin' *child* ... (**Levene** *has come out
during the diatribe with* **Lingk** *and has sat at the back listening. To*
Levene.) Don't leave. I have to talk to you. (*To*
Williamson.) You fucking *child* ... (**Roma** *goes into the inner
room.*)

Levene You *are* a shithead, Williamson ... (*Pause.*)

Williamson Mmm.

Levene You can't think on your feet you should keep your
mouth closed. (*Pause.*) You hear me? I'm *talking* to you. Do
you hear me ... ?

Williamson Yes. (*Pause.*) I hear you.

Levene You can't learn that in an office. Eh? He's right.
You have to learn it on the streets. You can't *buy* that. You
have to *live* it.

Williamson Mmm.

Levene *Yes*. Mmm. *Yes. Precisely. Precisely.* 'Cause your
partner *depends* on it. (*Pause.*) I'm *talking* to you, I'm trying to
tell you something.

Williamson You are?

Levene Yes, I am.

Williamson What are you trying to tell me?

Levene What I was trying to tell you yesterday. Why you
don't belong in this business.

Williamson Why I don't ...

Levene You listen to me, someday you might say, 'Hey ...'
No, fuck that, you just listen what I'm going to say: Your

partner *depends* on you. Your partner . . . a man who's your 'partner' *depends* on you . . . you have to go *with* him and *for* him . . . or you're shit, you're *shit*, you can't exist alone . . .

Williamson (*brushing past him*) Excuse me . . .

Levene . . . excuse you, *nothing*, you be as cold as you want, but you just fucked a good man out of six thousand dollars and his goddam bonus cause you didn't know the *shot*, if you can do that and you aren't man enough that it gets you, then I don't know what, if you can't take *some thing* from that . . . (*Blocking his way*.) you're scum, you're fucking white-bread. You be as cold as you want. A *child* would know it, he's right. (*Pause*.) You're going to make something up, be sure it will *help* or keep your mouth closed.

Pause.

Williamson Mmm.

Levene *lifts up his arm.*

Levene Now I'm done with you.

Pause.

Williamson How do you know I made it up?

Levene (*pause*) What?

Williamson How do you know I made it up?

Levene What are you talking about?

Williamson You said 'You don't make something up unless it's sure to help.' (*Pause*.) How did you know that I made it up?

Levene What are you talking about?

Williamson I told the customer that his contract had gone to the bank.

Levene Well, hadn't it?

Williamson No. (*Pause*.) It hadn't.

Levene Don't *fuck* with me, John, don't *fuck* with me . . . what are you saying?

Williamson Well, I'm saying this, Shel: Usually I take the contracts to the bank. Last night I didn't. How did you know that? One night a year that I left a contract on my desk. Nobody knew that but *you*. Now how did you know that? (*Pause.*) You want to talk to me, you want to talk to someone *else* . . . because this is *my* job on the line, and you're going to *talk* to me: Now how did you know that contract was on my desk?

Levene You're so full of shit.

Williamson You robbed the office.

Levene (*laughs*) Sure!

Williamson What'd you do with the leads? (*Pause. He points to the* **Detective**'s *room.*) You want to go in there? I tell him what we know, he's going to dig up *something* . . . You got an alibi last night? You better have one. What did you do with the leads? If you tell me what you did with the leads, we can talk.

Levene I don't know what you are saying.

Williamson If you tell me where the leads are, I won't turn you in. If you *don't*, I am going to tell the cop you stole them, Mitch and Murray will see that you go to jail.

Levene They wouldn't do that.

Williamson They would and they will. What did you do with the leads? I'm walking in that door – you have five seconds to tell me: or you are going to jail.

Levene I . . .

Williamson I don't care. You understand? *Where are the leads?* (*Pause.*) Alright. (**Williamson** *goes to open the office door.*)

Levene I sold them to Jerry Graff.

Williamson How much did you get for them? (*Pause.*) How much did you get for them?

Levene Five thousand. I kept half.

Williamson Who kept the other half?

Pause.

Levene Do I have to tell you? (*Pause.* **Williamson** *starts to open the door.*) Moss.

Williamson *That* was easy *wasn't* it?

Pause.

Levene It was his idea.

Williamson *Was* it?

Levene I ... I'm sure he got more than the five, actually.

Williamson Uh huh?

Levene He told me my share was twenty-five.

Pause.

Williamson Mmm.

Levene Okay: I, look: I'm going to make it worth your while. I am. I turned this thing around. I closed the *old* stuff, I can do it again. *I'm* the one's going to close 'em. *I* am! *I* am! Cause I turned this thing a ... I can do *that*, I can do *anyth* ... last night. I'm going to tell you, I was ready to Do the Dutch. Moss gets me, 'Do this, we'll get well ...' Why not? Big fuckin' deal. I'm hoping to get caught. To put me out of my ... (*Pause.*) But it *taught* me something. What it taught me, that you've got to get *out* there. Big deal. So I wasn't cut out to be a thief. I *was* born for a salesman. And now I'm back, and I got my *balls* back ... and, you know, John, you have the *advantage* on me now. Whatever it takes to make it right, we'll make it right. We're going to make it right.

Williamson I want to tell you something, Shelly. You have a big mouth.

Pause.

Levene What?

Williamson You've got a big mouth, and now I'm going to show you an even bigger one. (*He starts toward the* **Detective**'*s door.*)

Levene Where are you going, John? . . . you can't do that,
you don't want to do that . . . hold, hold on . . . hold on . . .
wait . . . wait . . . wait . . . (*He pulls money out of his pockets.*) Wait
. . . uh, look . . . (*He starts splitting the money.*) Look, twelve,
twenty, two, twen . . . twenty-five hundred, it's . . . take it.
(*Pause.*) Take it . . . (*Pause.*) Take it!

Williamson No, I don't think so, Shel.

Levene I . . .

Williamson No, I think I don't want your money. I think
you fucked up my office. And I think you're going away.

Levene I . . . what? Are you, are you, that's why . . . ? are
you nuts? I'm . . . I'm going to *close* for you, I'm going to . . .
(*Thrusting money at him.*) Here, here, I'm going to *make* this
office . . . I'm going to be back there Number One . . . Hey,
hey, hey! This is only the beginning . . . List . . . list . . . listen.
Listen. Just one moment. List . . . here's what . . . here's what
we're going to do. Twenty per cent. I'm going to give you
twenty per cent of my sales . . . (*Pause.*) Twenty per cent.
(*Pause.*) For as long as I am with the firm. (*Pause.*) Fifty per
cent. (*Pause.*) You're going to be my partner. (*Pause.*) Fifty
per cent. Of all my sales.

Williamson What sales?

Levene What sales . . . ? I just *closed* eight-two *grand* . . . Are
you fuckin' . . . I'm *back* . . . I'm *back*, this is only the
beginning.

Williamson Only the beginning . . .

Levene Abso . . .

Williamson Where have you been, Shelly? Bruce and
Harriett Nyborg. Do you want to see the *memos* . . . ? They're
nuts . . . they used to call in every week. When I was with
Webb. And we were selling Arizona . . . they're nuts . . . did
you see how they were *living*? How can you delude yours . . .

Levene I've got the check . . .

Williamson Frame it. It's worthless.

Pause.

Levene The check's no good?

Williamson You stick around I'll pull the memo for you. (*He starts for the door.*) I'm busy now . . .

Levene . . . their check's no good? They're nuts . . . ?

Williamson Call up the bank. *I* called them.

Levene You did?

Williamson I called them when we had the lead . . . four months ago. (*Pause.*) The people are insane. They just like talking to salesmen. (**Williamson** *starts for the door.*)

Levene Don't.

Williamson I'm sorry.

Levene *Why?*

Williamson Because I don't like you.

Levene John: John: . . . my *daughter* . . .

Williamson Fuck you.

Roma *comes out of the* **Detective**'s *door.* **Williamson** *goes in.*

Roma (*to* **Williamson**) *Asshole* . . . (*To* **Levene**.) Guy couldn't find his fuckin' couch the *living-room* . . . Ah, Christ . . . what a day, what a day . . . and I haven't even had a cup of *coffee* . . . Jagoff John opens his mouth he blows my Cadillac . . . (*He sighs.*) I swear . . . it's not a world of men . . . it's not a world of men, Machine . . . it's a world of clock watchers, bureaucrats, office holders . . . What it is, it's a fucked-up world . . . there's no adventure *to* it . . . (*Pause.*) Dying breed. Yes it is. (*Pause.*) We are the members of a dying breed. That's . . . that's . . . I want to talk to you. I've wanted to talk to you for some *time* actually . . . seriously. Did you eat today?

Levene Me?

Roma Yes.

Levene No.

Roma No? Come on, we're going to swing by the Chinks, we got to talk.

Levene I think I'd better stay here for a while.

Roma Okay: Two things, then. One . . . I been thinking about this for a *month*, I said 'the Machine . . . There's a fellow I could *work* with,' never, isn't that funny? I never did a thing. Now: That shit that you were slinging on the guy today was *very* good, and excuse me it isn't even my *place* to *say* that to you that way; I've been on a hot streak, so big deal. What I'm saying, it was *admirable* and, so was the *deal* that you closed. Now listen: there's things I could *learn* from you – you see, I *knew* we'd work well together – Here's what I was thinking: we Team Up. We team up, we go out together, we split everything right down the middle . . .

Baylen *sticks his head out of the room.*

Baylen Mr *Levene* . . . ?

Roma . . . fifty-fifty. Or we could go down the street. You know, we could go *anywhere* . . .

Baylen Would you step in here, please . . . ?

Roma So let's put it *together*? Okay? (*Pause.*) Shel? Say 'okay'.

Levene (*pause*) Hmm . . .

Baylen Mr Levene, I think we have to talk.

Roma I'm going to the Chinks. You're done, come down, we're going to smoke a cigarette.

Levene I . . .

Baylen *comes over to him and forcefully leads him into the room.*

Baylen . . . get in the room.

Roma Hey, hey, hey, *easy* friend. That's the 'Machine'. That is Shelly The Machine *Lev* . . .

Baylen Come on. Get in the goddamn *room* . . .

Levene I . . .

Roma I'll be at the resta . . .

Baylen *and* **Levene** *have disappeared into the next room and the door is slammed. Pause.*

Roma Williamson: listen to me: when the *leads* come in . . . listen to me: when the *leads* come in I want my top two off the list. For *me*. My usual two. Anything you give *Levene* . . .

Williamson . . . I wouldn't worry about it.

Roma Well I'm *going* to worry about it, and so are you, so you shut up and listen. (*Pause.*) I GET HIS ACTION. My stuff is *mine*, whatever *he* gets, I'm talking half. You put me in with him.

Aaronow *enters.*

Aaronow Did they . . . ?

Roma You understand?

Aaronow Did they catch . . . ?

Roma Do you understand? My stuff is mine, his stuff is ours.

Williamson Mmm.

Aaronow Did they find the guy who broke into the office yet?

Roma No. *I* don't know . . .

Pause.

Aaronow Did the leads come in yet?

Roma No.

Aaronow (*settling into a desk chair*) Oh, god I hate this job.

Roma (*simultaneous with 'job', going out of the office*) I'll be at the restaurant.

Prairie du Chien

Characters:

A Porter
A Card Dealer
A Gin Player
A Storyteller
A Listener
The Listener's Son

The Scene:

The play takes place in a railroad parlor car heading west
through Wisconsin in 1910. The time is three a.m.

Prairie du Chien was first produced by 'Earplay' for National
Public Radio in April 1979, with the following cast, directed
by Daniel Freudenberger: Charles Durning, Jeff Goldblum,
Larry Block and Bruno Kirby.

Prairie du Chien was given its British première at the Royal
Court Theatre Upstairs on 9 June 1986, with the following
cast:

Card dealer	Michael Feast
Gin player	Jerome Flynn
Porter	Cyril Nri
Storyteller	Nigel Terry
Listener	David de Keyser
Listener's son	Billy Ehninger

Directed by Max Stafford-Clark

Note: Directions in brackets pertain to radio production.

[*Sound: The continuous lulling sound of a railroad journey. We listen a while.*]

(*Note: All voices, except where indicated, should be very subdued, as suited to three a.m.*)

[*Sound: Cards being shuffled. Sound: Train whistling approaching a crossing. Long. Long. Short. Long.*]

Dealer Cut.

Gin Player I pass the cut.

Dealer Right.

[*Sound: Cards being dealt.*]

One, one, Two, Two. Three and Three.

[*Sound: **Dealer** yawns.*]

Gin Player You tired?

Dealer No. And four and four. Five *five*, six *six*, and Seven *seven*, eight, *eight*, nine and *ten*.

Gin Player Good.

Dealer Three of diamonds. (*Yawns.*) He takes the three of diamonds.

[*Sound: **Porter** approaching.*]

(*Pause.*) And throws the king. (*Pause.*) Throws the cowboy.

Porter Yassuh. Anything else I can get you gentlemen?

Dealer No. Thank you.

Gin Player No.

[*Sound: Money jingling.*]

Dealer Here.

Porter Thank you very *much* sir.

Dealer Sure. Throws the K.

[*Sound:* **Porter** *retreating.*]

Gin Player Play.

Dealer Yah. (*Pause.*) I play the king right back. (*Pause.*) And I get the *heart* five. (*Pause.*) The five of hearts. What does that tell us? (*Pause.*) When he has taken the three diamonds? (*Pause.*) When he has took the three of dimes?

[*Sound: The door to the car opens. Rushes of air, etc. The door is closed. Sound: We follow the footsteps of the person who has just come in. As he walks down the aisle the conversation of the card players fades.*]

Gin Player It's your play.

Dealer Yes. Alright. You use that? (*Pause.*) Eh? That's what I thought. And plays the ten.

[*Sound: The footsteps stop.*]

Storyteller (*expels air*) *Cold* out there! (*In an undertone.*)

Listener I'll bet it is.

Storyteller Phew! The boy still asleep?

Listener Yep.

Storyteller I wish I could sleep like that.

Dealer (*in the background*) Jack.

Storyteller 'Specially on a *long* ride.

Listener Yes.

Storyteller A *night* train. (*Pause.*) Never *could* sleep. (*Pause.*) *Never* sleep. Where was I?

Dealer Take it.

Listener Up in Council Bluffs, I think.

Storyteller That's right. Now I was *telling* you I'm up in Council Bluffs.

Dealer The six of diamonds. Six of diamonds and the five of hearts. Go on and take it. Take it, 'cause you *know* you want it.

Gin Player Well, I don't know if I want it yet, or not.

Storyteller . . . And this man owned a *drygoods* store. I'd see him five, six times a year when I'd swing through. Eh? Always good for a small order. Nothing great. But steady.

Listener Right.

Storyteller He had a lovely little wife.

Listener A young man.

Storyteller In his fifties.

Listener Uh-huh.

Storyteller In his fifties. (*Pause.*) And married two years at the time, perhaps. At that time that I speak of. (*Pause.*) He had a small farm out of town.

Listener Yes.

Storyteller (*pause*) He might have *been* something back East. But I don't know exactly. No one knew. Not even afterwards.

Dealer Four.

Gin Player You're going down with four?

Dealer Yes. Yes. I think I am.

Storyteller And his wife?

Listener Yes?

Storyteller My *God* she was a pretty thing.

Listener Mmm.

Storyteller And he was a jealous man. A very jealous man. Of money, too. Very tight-fisted. Always thought that he was being cheated. I can tell you. Smart, though. (*Pause.*) A clever man. (*Pause.*) There was talk he'd been a lawyer in the East.

Listener Mmm.

Storyteller And he was always bitter. As if he'd come *down*, you know? (*Pause.*) As if he'd come *down*, in life. (*Pause.*) Very

bitter. *She* was kind, though. (*Pause.*) To me. A lovely
woman. (*Pause.*) When I'd come through. If she was in the
store. They lived out on the farm. I told you?

Listener Yes.

Storyteller Just out of town. Him and their hand and her.
(*Pause.*) And she was just not happy. When I saw her. As the
months went by. I saw her fade. (*Pause.*)

[*Sound: The slap of cards.*]

(*The* **Storyteller** *sighs.*) And then one time when I came in.
(*Pause.*) And this is what I told you. (*Pause.*) I saw the welts.

[*Sound: From the back of the car we hear low whistling: 'The Banks
of The Wabash'.*]*

(*Pause.*) I saw bruises on her face and hands.

Listener Mmm.

Storyteller I had just come in. One day in March. She
came up to the store. She had been driven by their hand. This
colored man. He stayed down in the wagon and she came
inside.

Listener When was this?

Storyteller Spring. March. Sometimes warm. Disturbing.
Wet. One day cold, this one warm. I could see she was
disturbed. She drew him in the corner. They had you know,
they had words. He turned to me: 'What are you looking at?'
he says. And there was *hate* in his eyes . . . ?

Listener Mmm.

Storyteller I mean to tell you. (*Pause.*) And then he took to
ask me when I'd come in, had I seen his *wife*. (*Pause.*) Had I
seen her on the street . . . in any other town . . . He said: 'I
worry when I'm not at home', his eyes, he had this tone,
sarcastic, and you never knew if he was serious or what.
(*Pause. Mimicking.*) 'Have you seen my *wife*?' In town they

*See special note on copyright page.

told me he would check the buggy horses in the evening when he got home to see were they *tired*. (*Pause.*) If they'd been *out*.

Listener Why didn't he ask the hired man?

Storyteller He didn't trust him. Not by this time. Not at all.

Dealer (*faintly*) You know you want it.

Storyteller No. (*Pause.*) He was sure that she was stepping out on him. He had seen, he said that he had seen. (*Sotto.*) Is the boy asleep?

Listener Yes.

Storyteller *Traces* ... (*Pause.*) Eh?

Listener Yes.

Storyteller And he knew that she had been unfaithful. (*Pause.*)

Dealer You know you want it. Soo-cide jacks, Man with the Ax. Go on and take it.

Storyteller He knew she was stepping out. I'll tell you: one day my route brought me back. When I was swinging back I come in to the store. He has a *grin* on his face? (*Pause.*) Such a strange grin.

Listener Mmm.

Storyteller Not healthy. Not at all. In August. (*Pause.*) Dust in the air. (*Pause.*) Murder in the air. (*Pause.*) You could feel it. Animals could feel it. (*Pause.*) I tried to pass the time of day with him. He couldn't hear a word I said. 'What is it, friend?' I said. 'What's on your mind?' 'I'm going to kill my wife,' he says.

Dealer He takes the four.

Storyteller 'I'll tell you,' he says. 'If you ask. She's going to have a child. It isn't mine. And I am going to kill her.' (*Pause.*) 'She's going to tell me who the father is, and then I'll kill her.' Well. (*Pause.*) I tried talking to the man. I tried to keep him there. But he would not be held. We struggled. I don't think it was a contest. He was full of strength from hate. He hit me with something. He knocked me down. (*Pause.*) When I got up he was gone. (*Pause.*) I went for the sheriff.

[*Sound: Whistling stops.*]

Listener Were you hurt?

Storyteller I was not hurt. No. No. I found the sheriff. And I told him. Just what I told *you*. We rode out to the farm. From on a crest, about a half a mile out we saw a glow. The farm was burning. In the dusk. The barn was burning. We rode to the house. What did we see? (*Pause.*) On the porch. The farmer. Hanging from the crossbeam. Dead. His shotgun on the ground.

Listener He hung himself?

Storyteller Wait. And we heard. What sounded like a woman crying. In the house. (*Pause.*) Softly crying. Softly. (*Pause.*) The sheriff went inside. (*Pause.*) Cautiously. I waited on the porch. (*Pause.*) I heard voices. (*Pause.*) I heard, it sounded like: 'Go to the barn.' A woman's voice. 'Go to the barn. Please. Help him.'

Gin Player Twelve.

Dealer And three from twelve is nine.

Storyteller So I went to the barn. (*Pause.*) Burning. Burning. Through the doorway I could see the hired man. (*Pause.*) He was dead. (*Pause.*) Lying in the middle of the barn. He had a harness in his hand, and he had had a pitchfork stuck right up beneath his heart. (*Pause.*) And he'd been cut. His overalls were ripped down and the man had cut him. (*Pause.*) It was sickening. Five feet away there was the woman. In this lovely dress. This red dress. On her face. Her back was blowed away. And both of 'em are dead. (*Pause.*) And the barn's about to go.

Dealer You want it? Do you want the card?

Gin Player Yes.

Storyteller And the barn's about to go. (*Pause.*) Well, I start back to the house. Eh? On the way I meet the sheriff coming down. He says, 'Come on. The nigger's in the barn.' 'I know,' I say. 'He's dead.' 'You sure he's dead?' the sheriff says. 'Yes,' I say. 'Yes. I'm sure. Her, too. The both of 'em are dead.' 'Who?' he says. 'Both of who?' 'Him and the wife. The hand and her. He's killed 'em both.' 'No.' (*Pause.*) He says. 'Don't tell me that she's dead. Don't tell me that she's dead when I just saw her in the house.' 'Saw who?' 'The wife. Mrs McGurney,' he says. 'In the house. She told me to come down here. (*Pause.*) She told me to look in the barn.' 'Well, someone's dead,' I say. 'Him and a woman. Some white woman.' We run to the barn. And he is talking to himself. He's mumbling, 'She told me to come *down* here. No. To help the nigger.' (*Pause.*) We get there, barn's about to go now, any second. Cinders in the air as big as your hand. We stood in the door. The sheriff shouts 'Hallo!' The smoke blows. There they are. The two of them. (*Pause.*) In the middle of the barn. He's on his back. And she, I don't know, she has *crawled* to him. I would have sworn that she was dead. (*Pause.*) She has *moved* to him, and she has got her head upon his chest. 'That's her!' he says. 'That's her!' 'That's *who*?' (*Pause.*) I said. 'Who?' And then the barn caved in.

Gin Player Porter!

[*Sound:* **Porter** *approaches.*]

Porter Yassuh?

Gin Player What time is it?

Porter Two fifty-three, sir.

Gin Player Thank you.

[*Sound:* **Porter** *retreats.*]

Storyteller 'That's who?' I said. 'Mrs McGurney.'

Dealer Okay, then. That's sixty that you owe me, sixty, sixty-two, we'll call it sixty.

Gin Player Thank you.

[*Sound: Humming 'Redwing'*.]*

Storyteller   'Now wait,' I say. 'Wait. Didn't you just say you saw her in the *house?*' (*Pause.*) There was something in the air then. (*Pause.*) As if the air got thick. The barn was so hot. We fell back. The sheriff's shaking. He started to walk. To go back to the house. There was a smell like, I don't know. Like sweat. Like sick sweat. Do you know? We went back. (*Pause.*) And we went in. And all the time he mumbled to himself. 'No. No.' (*Pause.*) Very softly. We went in. And room by room we searched the house. We started in the cellar. There was no one there. (*Pause.*) There was no one there. In the whole house. (*Pause.*) We searched every room. Up to the attic. (**Listener** *makes a shivering sound.*) He'd seen her. (*Pause.*) He said he'd seen her. I heard something. (*Pause.*) And I would swear to that. But he said that he'd seen the woman. There was nothing in the house. Until as we were coming down the attic stairs. 'Look. Look!' he said. Then I saw something. To this day I could not tell you what it was. A form. (*Pause.*) Something blowing. I don't know. 'It's *her!*' he says. It went into the bedroom. Something went. I don't know. (*Pause.*) The door slammed. (*Pause.*)

Dealer   You deal.

Gin Player   *High* card deals.

Dealer   I'm sorry. You are absolutely right.

[*Sound:* **Porter** *enunciates first line of chorus softly. 'Now the Moon shines tonight on Little Redwing . . .', continues humming.*]

Storyteller   We went in. Through the bedroom door. (*Pause.*) We opened the bedroom door. (*Pause.*) There was no one in the room. The window was down and locked. (*Pause.*) There was only one door in the room besides the one we came in through. And it went to the closet.

Dealer   Nine and nine and ten and ten and three of diamonds.

*See special note on copyright page.

Storyteller And we stood there. (*Pause.*) He cocked his gun. (*Pause.*) And he motioned me to stand to one side. (*Pause.*) Well, my friend, I began to pray.

Gin Player Five.

Storyteller He moved to pull the closet door back. Then the door *behind* us was flung open. Well, we spun around. There were these three men from the town. (*Pause.*) Gaping at us. 'Get out!' they said. 'Get out 'cause she's coming down!' The house had caught a cinder from the barn. 'Get out!' they said. 'She's burning!' 'No, I'm *coming* out,' he says. 'I'm *coming* out. I'm checking.' 'Well, you *best* get out,' they said. And they went. We could hear them going through the house. 'Haloooo! Is anybody there?' (*Pause.*) 'Is anybody here?' He locked the door. He locked us in the room. He looked at me, and then he locked us in the room. And he stared at the closet. I heard something. I think that I heard something. It could have been the wind. (*Pause.*) It could be crying. Softly crying. In the closet. (*Pause.*) He grasped the handle, and he threw it open. There was no one there. (*Pause.*) It was empty. Except for this dress. This pretty red dress. (*Pause.*) And it was burning. (*Pause.*) The hem was burning. All around. As if that it had just been lit. The flames were rising. 'For the love of God, let's leave here,' I said. 'Please.' 'Oh *no*!' (*Pause.*) He was moaning to himself. 'No!' The room was full of smoke. I had to drag him from the closet door. 'Come on, man. For God's *sake* come on . . . !' (*Pause.*) I met the townsmen on the stairs. 'You have to help me,' I said. 'He's had too much smoke.' We dragged him from the house. The house was burning down, the barn was gone. (*Pause.*) The two bodies still inside. We watched the rafters fall. The night was gray. It was a strange, gray color, and the air was full of smells. We left the sheriff by the house. When we came back he was asleep. We woke him up. We all were going back to town. (*Pause.*) There was going to be an autopsy.

Listener On the storekeeper.

Storyteller On him, yes. He was the only one. We all gave depositions at the courthouse. This is what he said. 'I have been sleeping.' This is what the sheriff said. 'I have been sleeping. We rode out there. He was hanging. They were dead inside the barn.' And then he went to sleep. (*Pause.*) In the courthouse. (*Pause.*) He could not stay awake.

Dealer Twelve.

Gin Player And twenty's thirty-two.

Storyteller He could not stay awake. And they thought he was ill. But there was nothing wrong with him.

Gin Player Deal.

Storyteller Three years later he was killed.

Listener The sheriff.

Storyteller From the night the barn burned he was never right. They told me. When I came through. (*Pause.*) *Never* right. He slept the whole time. (*Pause.*) His wife deserted him. (*Pause.*) He lost his job, of course.

Listener Yes.

Storyteller He was not well. (*Pause.*) And then this man caught him. There had been *stories* . . . Is the boy asleep?

Listener Yes. (*Pause.*)

Storyteller There had (*Whispering.*) been those *stories* . . . and then this man caught him with his daughter.

Listener Caught the sheriff with his daughter.

Storyteller Yuh.

Listener How old was she? (*Pause.*)

Storyteller Ten. (*Pause.*) Ten years old.

Listener No!

[*Sound: Train approaches crossing and whistle hoots. Long, long short long.*]

Storyteller Yes. He told him, listen to this: 'I am going to take my daughter home. You tell me where you're going to be. Because I have to talk to you.' The sheriff told him he would be at home. (*Pause.*) Eh?

Listener Yes.

Storyteller Ten years old. (*Pause.*) And the man went to his house. He went in. He called. This is what I'm told. (*Pause.*) There was no one there. (*Pause.*) He heard someone rocking. On the floor above. (*Pause.*) Rocking in a chair. He heard the squeaking. He went up. He threw the door back and there was the sheriff. In a rocking chair.

Dealer He takes the jack, he doesn't take the ten.

Storyteller There is the sheriff dressed in a red dress. (*Pause.*) A red gingham dress. (*Pause.*) Rocking. (*Pause.*) He said, 'Please help him. They are in the barn. (*Pause.*) Help him. Please.' (*Pause.*)

Dealer Eight.

Storyteller 'Please help him.'

Gin Player You call with *eight*? The hell you say! (*Pause.*) Lay them down. Just lay them down and let's see what you've got.

Storyteller In a red gingham dress. (*Pause.*) 'Help him. Help him. Please.'

Dealer Here, count 'em up yourself.

Gin Player I will, yes thank you.

Dealer Have you had enough?

Gin Player What? No.

Storyteller Dressed like a lady. Eh? And rocking back and forth.

Listener What happened to the animals?

Gin Player Cut for the deal.

Storyteller What animals?

Dealer Six.

Gin Player Four.

Dealer Six deals.

Listener The *animals*. (*Pause*.) In the barn.

Storyteller *McGurney's* barn.

Listener Yes.

Storyteller What about them? You mean when the *barn* burned.

Listener Yes. (*Pause*.)

Storyteller What about them.

Listener Were they in the barn.

Dealer Six *six*, and seven *seven*, eight and eight . . .

Storyteller Yes.

Dealer Nine and ten and king of clubs.

Listener Why didn't they die? (*Pause*.)

Storyteller Well, I guess they *did*. (*Pause*.) I guess that they *did*. (*Pause*.) I guess that they *did*.

Dealer He takes the three of clubs.

Storyteller The horses and the cows . . .

Gin Player May I please see your cards?

Storyteller (*to himself*) All dead . . .

Dealer I'm sorry . . . ?

Gin Player May I see your cards?

Dealer You want to see my cards.

Gin Player Yes.

Storyteller (*to himself*) Yep, yep, yep, yep, yep.

Dealer Why do you want to see my cards?

Gin Player Just put 'em down.

[*Sound: Way back in the car the* **Porter** *has started humming to himself 'Meet Me In St Louis'.*]*

*See special note on copyright page.

Dealer I . . . wait. I want to tell you something.

Gin Player Lay your cards down.

Dealer I've got ten cards in my hand, friend. Same as you.

Gin Player I'm asking nicely. (*Pause.*) I want to see your hand.

Dealer And what if I don't want to show it to you? (*Pause.*) I'm not cheating you, friend. (*Pause.*) I'm not cheating you.

Gin Player (*raising his voice*) Count your cards. Just lay 'em down and count 'em.

Dealer (*pause*) Alright. One. Two. Three. Four, five, six. (*Pause.*) Seven. (*Pause.*) Eight. (*Pause.*) Nine, ten. Eh? Are you satisfied. You owe me eighty-seven dollars. (*Pause.*) It's time to settle up.

Gin Player I want to play some more.

Dealer You do?

Gin Player (*pause*) Yes.

Dealer (*pause*) Alright.

Storyteller So where you folks coming from?

Listener Chicago.

Storyteller Mmm. (*Pause.*) Where you going to?

Listener Duluth.

Storyteller The boy in school?

Listener Yes.

Storyteller Mmm. (*Pause.*) Fine-looking boy.

Dealer Cut for the deal.

Storyteller Up to Duluth, eh?

Listener Yes.

Gin Player Five.

Dealer A doctor. King of hearts. I deal.

[*Sound: Sound of train changes slightly.*]

Porter (*to himself*) We coming down the hill for water. Five minutes we be crost the bridge. I always tell it by the soun'.

Dealer And two and two and three and three. (*Pause.*) Four, four, five, five, the six and six and seven, seven, eight, eight, nine and ten. (*Pause.*) Two of spades.

Gin Player Pass.

Dealer I pass, too.

Storyteller (*to himself*) The skirt in flames around her ankles.

Dealer Two.

Gin Player Two. I take it.

Storyteller ... From the hem.

Dealer Three.

Storyteller ... Lapping up. As if that it had just been lighted.

Dealer Four. He drops the three, he drops the four.

Gin Player Just play.

Storyteller And sleeping with the hired man.

Dealer A stranger. Queen of clubs.

Storyteller ... The boy asleep?

Dealer The queen of clubs.

Listener Yes...

Storyteller Heavy with his child. (*Pause.*) They say.

Dealer Takes the queen.

Storyteller You can't know. Many things. You travel on a route up here.

Dealer He takes it.

Storyteller (*to himself*) *Many* things.

Dealer He takes the queen and throws the ten.

Storyteller They think that they can talk to you, 'cause they see you so seldom.

Porter (*to himself*) Slowin' down.

Gin Player (*yelling*) You son of a bitch! You're crimping *cards* on me! Don't touch that hand!

Dealer Now, wait. Now look: Look, we'll just throw it in. Just pay me what you owe me and let's quit. Alright. Look, we'll just throw it in . . .

Gin Player Don't you touch those cards you . . .

[*Sound: A pistol is fired twice.*]

Porter Oh, my sweet Jesus!

Boy Poppa!

Listener (*sotto*) Don't move. (*Pause.*)

Gin Player Did I hit you?

Dealer Oh, my God . . .

Storyteller Whyn't you give me that gun, mister. Whyn't you just hand it to me . . . ?

Gin Player Did I hit you? (*Pause.*)

Storyteller Why don't you give me the gun?

Gin Player Did I hit you?

Dealer No.

Storyteller Give me the gun. That's good. Give me the gun. Good. (*Pause.*)

Listener Did he hit the man?

Storyteller No. Now you sit down. Just sit down. Good, now.

Boy Poppa . . . ?

Listener It's alright.

Boy What happened?

Listener Nothing. These men had a fight. (*Pause.*) It's alright. Go back to sleep. (*Pause.*) Everything's alright now.

Boy Where are we?

Listener You go to sleep. We have a long long time to go yet.

Gin Player He. (*Pause.*) He was cheating me.

Dealer No one was cheating you. You're *crazy*, friend. (*Pause.*) Eh? You're *crazy*, fellow.

Gin Player He was crimping cards.

Dealer Where? Where? Show me one card. Show me one card marked. (*Pause.*) Eh? You son of a bitch. They ought to lock you up. They ought to take a *strap* to you. (*Pause.*) If you can't lose, don't *play*.

Gin Player (*pause*) I'm sorry.

Dealer Well, you owe me eighty-seven dollars here. (*Pause.*)

Gin Player Yes. Yes.

[*Sound: Train whistles. Sound: Train begins to slow down.*]

Here. Yes. Thank you.

[*Sound:* **Porter** *walking through car.*]

Porter Water stop. This. Prairie du Chien. Just about five minutes. Anybody want to stretch they legs we taking on some water.

[*Sound: Train whistle.*]

Gin Player Eighty. Eighty-five. Six. Seven.

[*Sound: Train coming to a stop. Blowing off of steam.*]

I'm sorry.

Porter Prairie du Chien.

Dealer Get me my bag, eh?

Porter Yassuh.

[*Sound: Bag being taken from rack. Panting. Sound: Progress of* **Porter** *and* **Dealer** *walking through car with bags.*]

Porter I got it, you just watch your step, suh, getting down. (*Pause. We listen to the sounds of the train taking on water, cooling, etc.*)

Storyteller Well! (*Pause.*) Well, I think that I'll step down and get some air. (*Pause.*) Join me?

Listener (*softly*) Son? (*Pause.*) Son? (*Pause.*)

Storyteller Is that boy asleep again?

Listener Son?

Storyteller Can you beat that? (*Pause.*) I'd give a lot to sleep like that. (*Pause.*) Yes, I would. Yessir, I would.

[*Sound: We listen to the sound of the train for a moment.*]

The Shawl

Characters:

John, *a man in his fifties*
Miss A, *a woman in her late thirties*
Charles, *a man in his thirties*

The Scene:

John's office.

The Shawl was first presented on April 19 1985 by the
Goodman Theater's New Theater Company in Chicago as
the première production of their Briar Street Theater, with
the following cast:

John	Mike Nussbaum
Miss A	Lindsay Crouse
Charles	Gary Cole

Directed by Gregory Mosher

The Shawl was given its British première at the Royal Court
Theatre Upstairs on 9 June 1986, with the following cast:

John	David de Keyser
Miss A	Connie Booth
Charles	Michael Feast

Directed by Richard Eyre

Act One

John *and* **Miss A**.

John ... You see:

Miss A I don't know ...

John Well, there is a rhythm in our lives, and at each point, at each point each of us should be doing that thing which corresponds to this rhythm. (*Pause.*) When you awaken it is to be brusque, to ... to be hungry (*Pause.*), to cleanse your mind for new impressions. (*Pause.*) To be acquisitive. At night it is appropriate to *think*, to meditate. And so it is with your life. (*Pause.*) You have a problem. What does this mean? In your life, in your day, in your ... as each one has his rhythm ... you ... and so *you* do. For we look at the stars. As they did. What do we see? We see this: that they named the constellations on their knowledge of the traits which appear in that ...

Miss A In ... ?

John In that period. You see? It was the *period* that they observed. How the *moon* ... (*Pause.*) How the *moon*, for example ... *influences* us. Influences *planting, reaping*. How in *our* lives we are influenced. At one time in your life. At most times, perhaps, you would, you would not be here. Would you? (*Pause.*)

Miss A No.

John No. Of course not. So we say, what is it that troubles you? And that you probably desire that I *inform* you. Is this not so?

Pause.

Yes?

Miss A I don't understand.

John I think you do. You've come to me for help. You wish me to resolve your 'problem'. First, though, you would like me to inform you what that problem is.

Miss A I...

John Is that not correct – to surmise ... it's alright ... to 'guess' ... you want me to exhibit my *power*. Is this not the truth? Is this not so? It is so. You wish me to, in effect, 'read your mind'. (*Pause.*) For the question is: WHAT POWERS EXIST? And what powers DO exist? And what looks after us? And ... do you see? This is a rational concern. *Is* there an order in the world. And ... you ask ... and *can* things be known. *Can* things be known. (*Pause.*) And, of course, they *can*.

Miss A ... they can.

John Of *course* they can, as you have suspected. (*Pause.*) Have you not?

Miss A Have I suspected it ...?

John Yes. And you have. For I see that *you* have ... *you* have some psychic ability.

Miss A I do...

John And you have *felt* it. Yes. You have. Questioned it. But felt it. Said it was ... *Answer* me, now ... You said it was ... you said it was ...? Have one moment's faith. Answer me. You said it was ...?

Miss A Coincidence.

John Exactly. But it was not. When you felt it. In those instances you know that I refer to. And you know the power of which I speak. (*Pause.*) *Don't* you. (*Pause.*) *Don't* you?

Miss A Yes.

John I know you do. And it *is* real. As we know it is real. And why should we be frightened? To *know* ...? And it is *better* to know. (*Pause.*) For we say 'knowledge', what is it? It is our attempt to be part of something which continues. Which we *are* part of. And *fear* – what is it? We fear that thing that we wish does not exist. But we know it exists. Don't we? (*Pause.*)

Miss A I don't know.

John Yes, you *do*. For what has brought you here? That knowledge. That there is a hidden order in the world. And once you dreamed this. You . . . you sat and dreamed this meeting with me. Long ago.

Miss A I did . . .

John *Dreamed* this when you were young . . . isn't that so? Isn't that so – *long* ago. Dreamt that you would one day sit with me. Didn't you? (*Pause.*)

Miss A Yes.

John I know that you did. In summer. When you were a little girl. Late summer. Sitting on a – what is it? By . . . is it by the *water* . . . ?

Miss A Yes.

John It *is*. Where is this?

Miss A At . . .

John At your home. Is it not? At your summer . . .

Miss A (*simultaneously with 'summer'*) Yes. Our summer home.

John I see . . . you by a tree. An oak? You sat and dreamed this meeting.

Miss A Yes.

John And I see another time of psychic power. When, you might have said 'suspicion' . . . A suspicion warned you of catastrophe. Is that correct?

Pause.

Miss A Yes.

John I see that it is. And you were right, is this not . . . ?

Miss A Yes. I was.

John And I see *other* danger ... and I see ... (*Pause.*) When you were *young. Blood.* When you were *quite* young. A fall. And you bear the scar still. Twice in your life you have been near death. Once that you knew of, once that you did not. Now think of the times I am speaking of. (*Pause.*) Danger. When you were in grave danger. And you will *remember* what I mean, no, there is nothing to be frightened of. What is it? Please?

Miss A You said 'a scar'.

John That is correct. That is another time. A fall. But now: think back to ... a time of physical danger.

Miss A A ... I don't ... (*Pause.*)

John Yes? (*Pause.*) What?

Miss A Where is this scar?

John It is on your left knee. What is it? (*Pause.*)

Miss A Oh ...

John Yes?

Miss A I don't have a scar there. (*Pause.*)

John You are quite wrong. And I see that you have forgotten it. As it is small. Now: if you would – if you would ... if you would look now you'll see that scar. Would you like me to turn away?

Miss A I don't.

John (*simultaneously with 'don't'*) It's alright. As I see it's important to you. You want to say you don't mean to 'test' me ... But you must trust me. And I am going to turn away. You look, and you'll see the scar.

Miss A It's alright. I don't have to see the ... I *believe* ...

John (*simultaneously with 'believe'*) No. You *must* look. *Not* belief but truth. Truth. For it is there. And that answers your doubts.

Miss A I don't have a scar there.

John Then you will prove me wrong, and then you'll know. Isn't it better to know? (*Pause.*) A small scar on your left . . .

Miss A Oh.

John I'm sorry? (*Pause.*) I'm sorry.

Miss A I don't. I don't know what to say.

John . . . what to say . . . Tell me what you saw.

Miss A There is a scar. I have a scar on my knee.

John Yes.

Miss A I never knew it was there.

John (*simultaneously with 'was'*) Yes. A small scar. You were quite young. When you were small then it was large. And it was traumatic, and so you repress it. We repress so much. But it all casts its shadow, and the things which you would know are all in you and all . . . *available* to you. (*Pause.*) Now: I see a loss. And I see suffering in your life. I see a loss. I . . . either you or someone close to you has suffered a tragedy.

Miss A (*softly*) Yes.

John Please . . . ?

Miss A Yes.

John Recently.

Miss A Yes. The loss of my . . .

John Of your mother. Yes. (*Pause.*)

Miss A You see that?

John Wait a moment, now . . .

Miss A I . . . you *see* that . . . ?

John Please. Try to . . . just . . . try to relax your . . .

Miss A (*simultaneously with 'your'*) My *mother*.

John I know that you loved her very much. Don't speak. And I see, *further* . . . (*Pause.*) I see . . . we were speaking: of that time in summer. We were speaking. She was near you then. No. She was *in* the house. You. You sat by the water. That time that you *dreamed* this. She was nearby. It's alright. I promise you. You are safe now, no harm can come to you here. She was *near* to you that time that you dreamed this meeting.

Miss A Yes.

John And she came out and she smiled. Now (**Miss A** *starts to cry*.) it's alright. (*Pause.*) It's alright. It's *good*. For you *must* mourn her ... For she is very much with us now.

Miss A My ...

John Yes.

Miss A My *mother* ... you *see* her?

John I see her as she was, I sense her *through* you. Your ... images ... feelings ... I see that *time* ...

Miss A What does she look like?

John (*simultaneously with 'like'*) And I see a question in your mind. Which you will not phrase, and that question is – listen to me for I am going to answer it; that question is this – and you must not feel foolish; that question is: (*Pause.*) can one contact her? Can she be contacted. (*Pause.*) Although that is not the thing that has brought you here. But it arises. Can one raise the dead. (*Pause.*) Now; do you wish to know that? (*Pause.*) Answer me.

Miss A Yes.

John Yes. I know. For I see how many times in the day you have thought of her. *Longed* for her ... Moments in *childhood* which have returned ... loneliness ... (*Pause.*) In your deep grief. And the questions of the spirit rise. And troubled, you come here. And we will *lift* your troubles. And answer your doubts. As all is open. (*Pause.*) I would like you to come back tomorrow. And bring me a photograph of her. And now (for the time is not right for that *other* question) let us address that which brings you here today. In the midst of your grief. Where everything ... where so much, as we see, is pain. And

I see you've had *much* sorrow in your life. And yet ... and I see strength ... and you have borne through it.

Miss A I have ...

John (*simultaneously with 'I'*) You were going to say 'you have attempted to', but you *have* ... and you have survived. Your father ...

Miss A Died when I was ...

John And now you bear up beneath this double burden. And an active trouble comes to you. A *question* rises. Which has led you here. (*Pause.*) It concerns money. Is this not ...? (*Pause.*) Is this not?

Miss A Yes. How do you know?

John (*simultaneously with 'know'*) And I see a matter of the law. A legal ...

Miss A My ...

John It is your mother's will.

Miss A Oh, my god.

John Is this not ...? (*Pause.*)

Miss A Yes.

John And you have come to *ask* me. If you should contest the will.

Miss A How do you know that?

John I ... (*Pause.*) I ... (*Pause.*) You must ... (*Pause.*) Let us continue:

Act Two

Charles *and* **John**.

Charles She came in.

John ... More tea?

Charles Thank you.

John Quite good don't you think?

Charles Mmm.

John Scald the pot.

Charles As you say ...

John Yes. She came in.

Charles And – (*Pause.*) You said she wasn't married.

John Why? Why did I say that?

Charles Because ... she had no ring.

John She *had* no ring. But, no, that isn't why I said it. You see: it comes down to confidence. They'll *test* you. And you can do nothing till you have their trust. You watch their eyes ... I mentioned the word 'husband' ... and her eyes did nothing. So we *confirm* she isn't married. Always confirm. (*Pause.*) They want to confess. Their question is: can They Confess to *You*? Can They Trust You. (*Pause.*) A woman. Comes to you ... she's troubled ... for why would they come if they were not? (*Pause.*) Eh?

Charles They wouldn't.

John No. So what do I do? What could trouble one? Anxiety. Or worry. Loss. And so I said, 'A tragedy'.

Charles You said, 'to you or someone close to you'.

John As who has not. You, you see? Seeming divination. Only common sense, and the idea of the *mystic* frees her to expound. Is this worth money? (*Pause.*)

Charles On which subject.

What do you have left?

John What?

Charles How much do you have left?

John Of? (*Pause.*)

Charles Of the fifty.

John Of the fifty she gave me?

Charles Yes.

John I have all of it left.

Charles . . . you . . . ?

John Yes?

Charles You have it all left?

John Yes.

Charles How did you buy the tea?

John Smiled at the Grocer's Boy. (*Pause.*) I opened an account.

Charles . . . you . . . ?

John Went down . . . on the strength of our new friend. I opened an account.

Charles And they let you?

John Yes.

Charles You didn't spend the fifty.

John (*simultaneously with 'fifty'*) How could I? The bill is for 'confidence'.

Charles For confidence.

John Yes. And I have to give it back to her tomorrow. She signed her name on it. You . . . I'd . . . I'd give it to you. But . . .

Charles . . . I didn't ask you for it . . .

John . . . but I have to give it back to her tomorrow. The same bill . . . What did I say?

Charles . . . you. I heard what you said.

John (*simultaneously with 'said'*) I said I told her, 'Let me have it to hold, and to meditate . . . '

Charles . . . I heard what you said.

John So – then we needn't . . . there'll be money . . . let's not . . .

Charles There'll be money when?

John Soon.

Charles And how will we 'get' this money. (*Pause.*) How will this money *come* to us?

John (*pause*) It will come to us. At the *end*. When she *asks*, 'How can I pay you?' We say, 'Leave something. To help us with our work. Leave what you will . . . ' They will ask and they will reward you. I told her to bring a photograph. Anything . . . Eh? This creates the habit. To bring something, to 'bring' things to you . . . their thoughts . . . 'money' . . . and when you don't *misuse* it, it creates confidence in them. And *when* we've helped her . . .

Charles *When* we've *helped* her . . .

John Yes. These things take time.

Charles (*simultaneously with 'time'*) When we've helped her to *what*?

John I've told you. To . . . to do whatever that is she wants to do. To . . . *face* herself . . . as we *will* help her . . . and she *will* reward us. And we're *making* progress. As you saw.

Charles I saw.

John Well, yes. You ... you ... she was won over. Didn't you see that?

Charles (*simultaneously with 'see that'*) Perhaps.

John Oh, no. SHE WAS WON OVER. She gave me the bill. She's going to bring the picture ... slowly ... slowly ... you can't force the ...

Coming to the Truth ...

(*Pause.*) Don't you see that?

Charles (*simultaneously with 'that'*) You said she dreamed this meeting.

John ... Ah. Did she foresee the meeting? We all dream of a wise man, one day ... who will ... I paint a picture. Looks like magic. You see her economic class ... by the way: look at the shoes, anyone could buy a pricey dress ... and we so we see an income of a certain magnitude. Suggests a summer house. Where? By the water is the obvious bet. And we suggest the mother nearby, you see? As the mother is the thing that draws her here. She's on her mind ... and her mind ... *freed* by 'magic' ...

Charles ... her mind freed by magic ...

John Yes. By my 'clairvoyance'. Yes. Yes. Yes. You must give them a *mechanism*. To allow them to *trust* you. She wouldn't trust just 'anyone'. She comes in: 'Show me you have psychic powers.' Alright. 'Read my mind. Tell me my complaint.' Alright. I will. A troubled woman. Comes in. With a problem? What is it? It's *money* – illness – *love* ... That's all it ever is. Money, illness or love.

A deeply repressed woman. In her thirties. Unmarried ... as you say ... Matter of the Heart? No. *Illness*. Perhaps. Woman of an anxious nature, that is a good bet. But no. I say 'the fear of death'. Three times. And no reaction. In her eyes. And so. Health. No. Love. No. And that leaves 'money'.

Charles And you said 'the Law'.

John I said a legal problem. How's this money come to her, a wealthy woman, but there's *contracts* . . . some legal . . .

Charles You said 'her mother's will'.

John Yes. I did.

Charles How did you know that?

John It was a guess. And an educated guess. Technique takes you so far, and then once in a while . . .

Charles And that's all there . . . that's all there is. (*Pause.*)

John What?

Charles That's all there is to what you do.

John Well, I suppose we all want 'magic', but our job, our *real* job . . .

One moment. I'm sorry . . . (*Pause.*) I'm sorry. You were speaking of money. I . . . I . . . what am I seeing . . . something came into my . . . evening . . . evening . . . eveningwear? A (*Pause.*) I see, what are they? Some stone? . . . Sapphire?

Charles What is this?

John Someone . . . a gift . . . they were *yours* . . . a set of sapphire studs. They . . . parted from them . . . ? You . . . no . . . yes. Valuable set of studs. A . . . a . . . and your concern with money and . . . you pawned a set of Sapphire Studs. (*Pause.*)

Charles How do you know that?

John Two weeks ago . . . before we met. Did . . . did you do that?

Charles You . . . how could you know that?

John I saw the pawn ticket. In your wallet. You see? Very simple, really. (*Pause.*) If one is allowed to believe . . . Our job is not to guess, but to *aid* . . . to . . . to create an atmosphere . . . As I just did with *you* . . . to enable . . .

Charles What were you doing in my wallet?

John Well. The man came with the *food*, I had to *tip* him . . . you were in the *shower*, I'm *sorry*. I did . . . I *certainly*

Charles You should not have looked in my wallet.

John No, you're absolutely right. I should . . . I should not. I'm sorry. I'm *very* sorry. Charles. I'm *very* sorry. I took a *dollar*, the ticket fell . . . you're absolutely right. And I apologize. (*Pause.*) I apologize. Will you forgive me? (*Pause.*) Will you please forgive me? (*Pause.*)

Charles You're very nosy.

John Yes, I. And I suppose that it's a professional . . . you're *right*. And I apologize. And I'm sorry as it's obvious that it's a touchy . . .

Charles I should *say* that it's a 'touchy'. *Yes*. It. Well, I would say that it . . .

John We are going to have money. I *promise* you. When she comes to *us* asks *us*: 'How can I repay you?' We say, 'Leave what you will. To aid us in our work . . . Some would leave fifty, some would leave a thousand.' . . . We are going to . . .

Charles When?

John Soon.

Charles When?

John As soon as I start to catch on. Which will be soon. Which, trust me, and she is the first sign, and a certain sign. I promise you. And we'll have your *studs* back, and . . .

Charles . . . how long will it take?

John However . . . a short while.

Charles A short while.

John Yes. (*Pause.*) And what I *have*. (*Pause.*) What I have . . . whatever I have, whatever I have is yours.

Charles And just what is that now?

John Just now that's very little. In material things. Very little. What I *can* offer you is: a . . . a profession. The beginnings of a craft. Which would sustain you, which . . .

Charles A profession.

John *Yes*. It *is*. To *help* . . . to . . . And I see what it is that *upsets* you. For the lack of money is a *sign* . . .

Charles It is . . .

John That something . . . yes, it is . . . that something *valuable* is missing. You have lost something which causes you to doubt. (*Pause.*) And I *see now* why it is you're disappointed. For your question is this: how legitimate is that thing which I do.

Charles Is that my question?

John Yes. It is. Though you don't *know* it is. That's why you balk at these . . . I *show* you the trick 'from the back' and you're disappointed. Of course you are. If you view it as a 'member of the audience'. One of the, you will see, the most painful sides of the profession is this: you do your work well, and who will see it? No one, really . . . (*Pause.*) If you do it well. (*Pause.*) But . . . (*Pause.*) To say, to learn to say, I suppose you must, to just say what separates us, finally, from them is this: that is we look *clearly*. So be it. Not that we're 'special' . . . (*Pause.*)

Charles You told her that she was psychic.

John . . . I tell that to everyone . . . Not that we're 'mystic'. But that we can see. Those very things which are before our eyes. Look at her. (*Pause.*) She is unmarried. At her time in life. Why? She is bound. To what? An unresolved event. Her mother's death? Her question, she would ask the 'spirit world', her mother left a fortune to her stepfather. Should she contest this will in the courts. Is this a question for the mystic? No. It hides a deeper one: this: how can I face my betrayal. How can I obtain revenge. Against the dead. Or: why did my mother not love me more? And so we help her. To *answer* that *last* question.

Charles And how is it we do that?

John By telling her what she wants to know.

Charles And what is that?

John We don't know. We listen and she'll tell us ...
tomorrow. You'll listen again ...

Charles I will ...

John Yes.

Charles And how many days will I listen?

John How many ... ?

Charles What is this. A *month* ... a *year*? How many ...

John I told you ... As we gain her *confidence*.

Charles Her confidence. If it's a trade you should be paid
for it.

John We will.

Charles (*simultaneously with 'will'*) You doing something for
the girl or not? What are you frightened of ... ? Should you
be paid for this or not? Well, *I* should. *I* should. Cause I'm
sitting here, too.

(*Gets up.*) Where's the fifty.

John Fifty.

Charles Give me the bill.

John I can't. How can I? She *signed* it. I have to give it back
to her to ...

Charles What is this, a *child's* game? Give me the *bill*.

John No, No, No. I *can't*. If she comes back here and the bill
is gone ...

I see. I see. Charles. Charles. I see. That ... sit down, please.
I see that I've humiliated you.

Charles You have ... ?

John Over a 'Dollar'. Yes. For Nothing. For money. I went in your wallet. I see that you're *hurt* . . .

Charles You see that . . .

John Yes, and.

Charles Well, you see it all. *Don't* you? Tell me what else do you see? You see that she wanted to contact the Spirits. (*Pause.*)

John She, well, I *told* you that.

Charles Now: what did she want you to do?

John To throw a *seance*, to . . . you know, *effects* . . . miraculous . . . entities . . . unknown *facts* . . .

Charles Unknown facts?

John Facts only her mother could know.

Charles And people could give those to her?

John Of course.

Charles How?

John Uh, well, you just go to the library. Yearbooks. Society files . . . Research. You invent a 'contact'. Um. Some Spirit Medium. Lived in the Nineteenth Century. A friendly spirit gone before . . .

Charles And you could do this?

John I'm *telling* you. Once you have won their trust you . . .

Charles You've *done* it?

John No. I've *seen* it done. I've *seen* it done . . . What?

Charles You know what?

John No, no, that's why I asked you. What . . . what . . . what . . .

Charles We should use the tools that you've developed.

John I do – use them. What do you . . . in what way?

Charles We should take her fortune from her.

John Well, there are many who would.

Charles Then we should do it.

John Well. No. I don't think so. (*Pause.*) We all feel greed
... sometimes ... for those things we cannot have, or which
seem ... things *myself*, things that I want for *you*, for *us*, but if
we just correctly *understand* those ...

Charles You said that she wants a seance. And she's going
to have it. You said research. I want you to tell me the
research I should do. I'm going to do it. When she comes
tomorrow we'll give her her seance. You'll make her mother
suggest she should contest the will and then give us the
fortune.

John No.

Charles And you will *do* it or else I am leaving you. Do you
understand?

Pause.

Do you understand me?

John Would you force me to make that choice?

Charles I've done it. Now the choice is yours.

Act Three

John, Charles *and* **Miss A**.

John Are you comfortable?

Miss A Yes.

John Would you ... please remove your wristwatch, your *rings* and loosen anything which constricts the free flow of blood. Charles:

Charles Yes.

John Dim the lights, please. (*Pause.*) Thank you. (*Pause.*) Now: are you ready to begin?

Miss A Yes.

John May we be *silent* a moment, and open our minds to that thing which we hope to do. Not to strain, not to *seek*, but simply to *open* ourselves. Quietly. Yes. (*Pause.*) We are here today to attempt to make *contact*. With one recently departed. Whose *soul* lingers here. Who *is* here with us ... to attempt to *contact* her. To *ask* her: to address a question ... and we seek the aid. Of someone gone before. (*Pause.*) To aid us. As they've aided us before. Yes, That's right. Are you alright?

Miss A Yes. (*Pause.*)

John The candles, please. SPIRITI MEI INFERNALI OBEDITE. In the year eighteen forty-three there lived in Boston a shopkeeper named Hawks. Samuel Hawks. He kept a shop on Tremont Street. Who sold tobacco, who dealt with all aspects of society. A merchant captain who dealt with the store, who supplied him, who bought from him, who did business with Mr Hawks and who was invited to come to his home and who became a friend. Many's the time he came there and he was welcomed into the family; the captain came and told the stories of the sea. Won over, he won over her, she was wooed by his life and left her family to meet him. Afternoons by the docks, by the waterfront I went there to his room he rented and it smelt of sweat, the curtains blowing on the dock, we saw the curtains blow, the ship commands from down, men working men on the wharves, do your bidding on the sea but what's here? Used to native hands ways of the south which we cannot imagine in extremity they make an offer to their lord, some passion but the horror was he'd brought it home. I was won to the danger he would get away but how would I?

I would not. Immured in that house I prayed for when he'd come, what can you ask but that I gave it and he asked it and I did. I grabbed his hair and helped him to me, I cried out what I discovered was that I had the disease, take me with you. No and so when he went . . . how could I say? Even my children here, who'd asked him to come, but he came, 'you have ruined me'. And Take Me. No. Take me upon your ship. No. No. How can you leave me in this room – clung to him threatened, his fierce, my mistake, threatened with the . . . you say that I reaped the desired result, that I won, stabbed, stabbed in the belly, ripped out with his dirk, bloodied the sheets, wiped it upon the wall, which, when he went out, not to the ship but back to the store, to take leave, to close the contract, when he'd killed me . . . told my husband he left his regards, while I was staring at it. His esteemed wife. Who, the tide set, standing at the helm. Felt no remorse. Felt nothing. Said nothing. All those years. Died respected. He died. When they would not claim my corpse. The voices from the wharf. I saw the Bloodmark, I, then he went in that room. I knew the afternoon before my husband brought him home. But seated there . . . (*Pause.*) And the servant said the race has bred the smell out of itself . . . and so was dying in its bed. Laid in disgrace. Lured to the squalid room and killed. Everyone knew. It seemed everyone knew but me. And so you come to me.

Pause.

As others have. And ask me. Hidden from all but not from my pain.

I see a house. I see a white house.

(*Pause.*) I see a numeral.

Miss A What do you see?

John I see the number eight. A year . . . ?? I . . . An address . . . ? I see the figure 'eighty-four'.

Miss A Eighty-four. That . . .

John What?

Miss A That was our house on . . .

John (*simultaneously with 'our'*) Why do you come to me for help?

Miss A That was our house on Rosemont Street . . .

John (*simultaneously with 'Rosemont'*) A woman has died, a dress, she . . . A *party* dress. White. Off-white . . . rose . . . ?

Miss A A . . .

John A party dress. She gave you. That she bought . . . she bought it for you.

Miss A She bought in Paris.

John I see her there, and I . . . A night. What? You were, what?

Miss A When she kissed me.

John And I see her standing by your bed. She said. She said, 'You are my . . .'

Miss A (*simultaneously with 'my'*) 'You are my little . . .'

John I called to you.

Miss A When?

John I see her.

Miss A What do you see?

John I see her as she stood beside you. She is at your bed. A
... a ... a red brick building. She is in your room. She ... at
your door. A red brick building ...

Miss A (*simultaneously with 'building'*) That's my
apartment ...

John (*simultaneously with 'apartment'*) She ... you. Wait! You
felt her there ... last ... last ... *recently*. She *came* to you. She
says ...

Miss A I ...

John 'I *called* to you ...' 'Don't you *hear*??' When is this ...?

Miss A It's ... it's

John When ... when ...?

Miss A It's my *apartment* ...

John She stood ... don't you *hear* her? She stood by your
bed. She *called* you. Are you ... you asked, you prayed to her,
to come, to reveal ...

Miss A What, I ...

John You hear a knocking. Your mother, 'I called your
name.' But no faith. You *heard* her. She came to you, *say* it.

Miss A I ...

John Your apartment. And you heard a knocking at the ...

Miss A I don't ...

John Yes! You *heard* her! The *wind* blew. SHE WAS
CALLING YOUR NAME!!!

Miss A (*pause*) It was my name I thought ...

John You *know* it was. (*Pause.*) In your dream ... she said,
'What did you dream? And what did you dream that night?'
And you told her your dream. 'Sleep. For I am always with
you.' She said that to you. She called you. She *told* you. Oh.
Those times. Those years. She mourned. How she mourned.
How she ... for your ... for your grief, I've seen her. 'My
darling child ...' Dreamt of the ... stand, standing by the

bed, called ... 'My darling child'. And why do you resist me?
And she said you have a question. Something troubles ... ?

Miss A The ...

John 'I made a will ... ' The mon ... the money ... she left
... she has left it. To ... to someone *else*. She ... She's saying
... wait ... I ... (*Pause.*)

Charles ... go on ...

John I don't think I ... I'm losing ...

Charles Go on.

Miss A Will you please ...

John You have a photograph of her ... ?

Miss A I ...

John *Put* it. Face down on the table. 'As, Alif Casyl, Zaza,
Hit Mel Melat.' Place your hands on it. (**Miss A** *does so.*)
She ...

(*Pause.*) I've ...

I ... (*Pause.*) You have a question ... your dear mother ...
'Let this man decide.' The question of ... you're troubled ...
I ... I ... be assured she loves you ... She says be free of the
money. And you must forsake your ... She: 'I will never
leave you.' Your mother lives in you still. 'Follow my
counsel, and come again,' and

Charles ... she says ...

John (*simultaneously with 'says'*) She loves you still. She ... 'I
left you unwillingly ... ' And we will meet again ... I'm ...
(*Pause.*) I'm ... (*Pause.*) I see the shades, a mark upon the, she
is in the room by the dock, I feel ... (*Pause.*) I'm sorry.
(*Pause.*)

Charles Are you alright?

John I'm fine. I ... (*Pause.*) I'm fine. (*Pause.*) I need a
second. What did I ... ? Will you open the ...

He gestures **Charles** *to the windows, where the shades are opened.*

(*Pause.*) (*Sighs.*) It's gone. (*Pause.*)

Miss A And ... ? (*Pause.*) May I speak ... ?

John (*simultaneously with 'speak'*) You want to ... and the woman who spoke is that ... ? What happened? (*Pause.*)

Charles The Boston Woman.

John Yes. The Boston Woman spoke. She ... what did she ... ? A concern for ... she ...

Charles She said she made contact with the ...

John (*to* **Miss A**) With your mother.

Miss A Yes.

John She said that?

Miss A Yes.

John And?

Miss A She said, 'Let the man decide.'

John Let ... which means ... ?

Miss A To ...

John That *we* should decide. That *I* ...

Miss A Yes.

John That I should decide about the legal ...

Miss A Yes.

John I'm, I'm, I'm ... That was the question you addressed to her ... But not qualified, of course, I ...

Miss A You could ...

John I could what?

Miss A Ad ...

John Advise ... ?

Miss A You could advise me. (*Pause.*)

John (*sighs*) No. I don't ... I suppose I ...

Miss A You saw my mother. (*Pause.*)

John (*to* **Miss A**) The contact saw her. I retain a . . . dimly
. . . dimly . . .

Miss A Was she as you see her in this photograph?

John The photograph. Turn it up. (**Miss A** *does so*.) Yes.
Yes. She. Yes. (*Pause*.) She was somewhat *younger*. Your
mother. As I saw her in . . .

Miss A (*simultaneously with 'in'*) THAT'S NOT HER
PHOTOGRAPH. I TOOK IT FROM A BOOK. You're
all the, all of you, God *damn* you! How could you, 'I see her by
the bed'. How can you *prey* on me? Is there no *mercy* in the
world . . . ?

Charles If you . . .

Miss A If you can't *help* me, NO one can help me . . . why
did I *come* here. All of you . . . Oh *God*, is there no . . . how can
you *betray* me . . . You . . . you . . . God *damn* you . . . for
'money' . . . ? God . . .

Charles . . . get her out of here . . .

Miss A May you rot in hell, in *prison*, in . . . you *charlatan*,
you *thief* . . .

Charles We've . . .

John *No*. Oh God forgive me . . .

Miss A If there's any power in the world . . . (*Rising*.)

John No!

Miss A . . . I'm going to . . .

John Oh, God help me, I'm sorry . . .

Miss A GET OUT OF MY WAY!

John Oh, God Help Me. I see Your Sainted Mother.
Wrapped you in a Shawl. A Red Shawl . . . Which she
brought back, which she wore, she whispered, 'I Am Coming
Home . . .' When she went out. Your father took her. For the
evening. And. When she came home. Into your room, she
draped it on the lamp. It cast a red . . .

Miss A ...No.

John Yes. And she would sing to you, 'Are you asleep? My lamb ... ?' And she would sing, you hear her.

Miss A No.

John And she would cradle you. The shawl smelt of perfume. You lost it *when*? Five ... Five ...

Miss A Yes.

John What?

Miss A Five years ago.

John And told no one, and grieved, a yellow flower, a rose, in the middle, and a golden fringe, she sang, 'Are you asleep my lamb?' And she thinks of you still. And calls to you. And she calls to you now. And I saw her by your bed. She Wore The Shawl.

Act Four

John *and* **Charles**.

Charles Well. (*Pause.*) I suppose ... (*Pause.*) I suppose we ... (*Pause.*) I'd like to *stay* here. (*Pause.*)

John No. I ... I ... We've *done* that.

Charles I said I'd like to stay here.

John Yes. It cannot ...

Charles All you have to ...

John I wish it were so. It is not so, it is not all I ...

Charles What is it? You think you have to 'atone'? You ... ?

John I ... *I* ... No, you see, that I ... No. That's not it.

Charles I Want To Know.

John I'm sure you do.

Charles I want ...

John The things we want. Many things that I want ...

Charles I want to stay with you.

John And know the Question. 'How will the World End.' 'Will I Be Rich.'

Charles Don't force me to go.

John *Tricks*. Don't you ... ? Attracted. So attracted ... Ah ... you want to know a trick. And when I show you a trick ... 'But you read her mind.' (*Pause.*) Yes? I 'suggested' her. That's all I did. Eh? And now you can feel superior. And there is no mystery. And then you can go. 'The Secrets of the Pyramids'? No. I went to the library. Society files. Perhaps two pictures. Of a woman in a red-fringed shawl. Two different photos. Yes, a well-to-do woman. And what would one assume? She wore it often. She wore it out, and she wore it home. An anxious child, the child couldn't sleep. The mother wore it in the room. The child remembered it. Are you free now? Now that you know The Mysteries? (*Pause.*) The Pythagorean mysteries? (*Pause.*) The Sacred . . . ? (*Pause.*) Three cups. And which cup hides the ball . . . Well. No. You asked to . . . you . . . I have nothing to . . . I wish I . . . (*Pause.*) I . . . (*Pause.*) Are you content? (*Pause.*)

Charles Am I content?

John Will you . . . yes. Will you, you're now equipped to live in a world without mystery. And now you know all that I know. And now you may leave content. (*Pause.*)

Charles Wait. You said, 'a scar'.

John I . . . ?

Charles You said, 'a scar'. The first time she came. A scar. On her left knee. She didn't know it *herself*.

John A scar.

Charles And she didn't know it herself. How could you?

John One final mystery. She is right-handed. Now: as children we all fall. And, to break the fall a right-handed person falls on his left knee. Ninety percent of the right-handed people in the world have a small scar on their left knee. I'm sorry. (*Pause.*) Goodbye.

Charles You said we all must learn.

John Did I say that?

Charles Yes. And . . . yes. And . . . you've *shown* me . . . and . . . wait! You said she lost it five years ago. How . . .

John I TOLD YOU. IT WAS A *TRICK*. IT WAS A *TRICK*. ARE YOU *DEAF*? Live in the World. Will you, please? That's what *I'm* trying to do. I'd *wished* that we would be something more to each other. It was not to be.

Charles I . . .

John And so goodbye. I'm truly sorry to have disappointed you. (*Pause.*)

Charles I . . . (*Pause.*) Goodbye.

John Yes, we said that.

Pause. **Charles** *exits.* **John** *stands alone.*

John 'As, Alif Casyl, Zaza, Hitmel Meltat.' (**Miss A** *enters.*) Yes, yes, yes. Come in. I . . . is it time already . . . ? for our . . . ?

Miss A I'm a little early, may I . . . ?

John Please.

Miss A May I sit down?

John Please.

Miss A Thank you. (*Sits.*)

John How are you today?

Miss A I'm fine . . . I . . . are you alright?

John Perfectly.

Miss A . . . you seem . . . ?

John I was with a client, and you are absolutely right. Now: let me clear my mind, and . . . (*Pause.*) Yes. Now. You seem . . . you've *decided* something, for you seem in better *spirits* today. Something has been . . . And a *burden* has been lifted from your mind. Good. I see *clarity*. Good. For there's so much sorrow in this life. A question answered. For, finally, we must solve them all in our own mind. And we know that is true. (*Pause.*) Good. (*Pause.*) Yes. Yes. What? What is it? (*Pause.*)

Miss A I have to ask you something.

John . . . but still skeptical. Good. We can't overcome our nature. For it protects us. You ask what you wish to ask.

Miss A You won't be offended.

John No. I promise you.

Miss A If I were to ... (*Pause.*)

John Tell me. If you were to *what*?

Miss A If I were to search in *Boston*. For a Mister Hawks.

John Yes.

Miss A And for his *wife*, in 1840 who was murdered ...

John If you search then what would you find? That it was a story, that someone made up. That it was true? Then someone could have read it. That it was not noted, then perhaps it had been overlooked.

Miss A Mm.

John I see that's insufficient, but it must suffice. You see: it's not *divination* that concerns you. Finally. The question of your mother's will. And I see you've decided.

Miss A Yes. I'm going to contest the will.

John I think that that is what you want to do.

Miss A Yes. It *is*, it's exactly what I want to do. (*Pause.*) And I'd like to *thank* you. (*Pause.*)

John I'm glad to do what I can.

Miss A And I'd like ... how do I *pay* you?

John You may pay me what you wish. And when you wish.

Miss A ... what is the usual ...?

John Those, those that have been helped – some might, some, as they can afford it, as they wished, might pay up to a thousand dollars. To help us with our work. Some would leave fifty. Some would leave nothing. It's completely up to you. (*Pause.*)

Miss A You made contact with my mother.

John That is not the ...

Miss A You *contacted* her.

John Well. Perhaps I did. And ... I ... I ... I don't *know*.

Miss A You saw her. No. You saw her wrap me in that shawl. No one could know that. You *saw* her.

John *Did* I see her . . .

Miss A No. You must *tell* me. (*Pause.*) You *must* tell me. You *saw* her. (*Pause.*)

John Yes.

Miss A You saw her wrap me in that shawl.

John Yes. (*Pause.*)

Miss A And you say I *lost* it.

John You, yes, that is what I said. But you did *not* lose it. You *burnt* it. In rage. Standing somewhere by the water, five years ago.

Miss A Yes. And then I . . . ?

John I do not know. That is all I saw.

Speed-the-Plow

This play is dedicated to Howard Rosenstone

Which is the most reasonable, and does his duty best: he who stands aloof from the struggle of life, calmly contemplating it, or he who descends to the ground, and takes his part in the contest? 'That philosopher,' Pen said, 'had held a great place amongst the leaders of the world, and enjoyed to the full what it had to give of rank and riches, renown and pleasure, who came, weary-hearted, out of it, and said that all was vanity and vexation of spirit. Many a teacher of those whom we reverence, and who steps out of his carriage up to his carved cathedral place, shakes his lawn ruffles over the velvet cushion, and cries out that the whole struggle is an accursed one, and the works of the world are evil. Many a conscience-stricken mystic flies from it altogether, and shuts himself out from it within convent walls (real or spiritual), whence he can only look up to the sky, and contemplate the heaven out of which there is no rest, and no good.

'But the earth, where our feet are, is the work of the same Power as the immeasurable blue yonder, in which the future lies into which we would peer. Who ordered sickness, ordered poverty, failure, success – to this man a foremost place, to the other a nameless struggle with the crowd – to that a shameful fall, or paralyzed limb or sudden accident – to each some work upon the ground he stands on, until he is laid beneath it.'

— Thackeray,
Pendennis

Characters:

Bobby Gould, **Charlie Fox**, *two men around forty*
Karen, *a woman in her twenties*

Scenes:

Act One: Gould's office, morning
Act Two: His home, that evening
Act Three: His office, the next morning

Speed-the-Plow was first presented in a New York Broadway production by Lincoln Center Theater at the Royale Theater, opening on 3 May 1988, with the following cast:

Bobby Gould	Joe Mantegna
Charlie Fox	Ron Silver
Karen	Madonna

Directed by Gregory Mosher
Designed by Michael Merritt
Costumes by Nan Cibula
Lighting by Kevin Rigdon

This production subsequently transferred to the National Theatre, London, on 25 January 1989, with the following changes:

Bobby Gould	Colin Stinton
Charlie Fox	Alfred Molina
Karen	Rebecca Pidgeon

Act One

Gould's *office. Morning. Boxes and painting materials all around.* **Gould** *is sitting, reading,* **Fox** *enters.*

Gould When the gods would make us mad, they answer our prayers.

Fox Bob . . .

Gould I'm in the midst of the wilderness.

Fox Bob . . .

Gould If it's not quite 'Art' and it's not quite 'Entertainment', it's here on my desk. I have inherited a monster.

Fox . . . Bob . . .

Gould Listen to this . . . (*Reads.*) 'How are things made round? Was there one thing which, originally, was round . . . ?'

Fox . . . Bob . . .

Gould (*leafing through the book he is reading, reads*) 'A certain frankness came to it . . .' (*He leafs.*) 'The man, downcast, then met the priest, under the bridge, beneath that bridge which stood for so much, where so much had transpired *since* the radiation.'

Fox . . . yeah, Bob, that's great . . .

Gould Listen to this: 'and with it brought grace. But still the question persisted . . . that of the Radiation. That of the growth of animalism, the decay of the soil. And it said "Beyond terror. Beyond grace" . . . and caused a throbbing . . . machines in the void . . .' (*He offers the book to* **Fox**.) Here: take a page.

Fox I have to talk to you.

Gould Chuck, Chuck, Chuck, *Charles*: you get too old, too busy to have 'fun' this business; to have 'fun', then what are you . . . ?

Fox . . . Bob . . .

Gould What are you?

Fox What am I . . . ?

Gould Yes.

Fox What am I when?

Gould What are you, I was saying, if you're just a slave to commerce?

Fox If I'm just a slave to commerce?

Gould Yes.

Fox I'm nothing.

Gould No.

Fox You're absolutely right.

Gould You got to have fun. You know why?

Fox Okay: why?

Gould Because, or else you'll die, and people will say 'he never had any fun'.

Fox How close are you to Ross?

Gould How close am I to Ross . . . ? I don't know. How close should I be?

Fox I have to ask you something.

Gould (*pause*) Go ahead, Charl.

Fox You wanna greenlight a picture? What's your deal, what's your new deal?

Gould What's my new deal, that's all you can talk about?

Fox What's your new deal?

Gould Alright. Over ten mil I need Ross's approval. Under ten mil, I can greenlight it. So what. (*Pause.*)

Fox This morning, Bob.

Gould ... Yes ... ?

Fox This morning a man came to me.

Gould ... a man came to you. Whaddayou, already, you're here to 'Promote' me ... ?

Fox Bob ...

Gould You here to promote me? Charl? Because, Charl, one thing I don't need ...

Fox Bob.

Gould When everybody in this jolly *town* is tryin' to promote me, do you wanna see my messages ... ?

Fox Bob.

Gould 'Get Him While He's Hot' ...

Fox Yes, yes, but ...

Gould My good, my 'good' friend, Charles Fox ...

Fox Bob ...

Gould That's why we have 'channels'.

Fox Uh huh.

Gould All these 'little' people out there, that we see. Y'unnerstand? Fellow asks 'what are they *there* for?' Well, Charl, We Don't Know. But we *think*, you give the thing to *your* boy, gives it to *my* boy, these people get to *eat*, they don't have to go *beg*, and get in everybody's face the *airport* the whole time. This morning the phone won't stop ringing. Do you know who's calling? Everybody says they met me in *Topeka*, 1962, and do I want to make their movie. Guys want me to do remakes of films haven't been made yet.

Fox ... Huh, huh ...

Gould I'm drowning in 'coverage'. (*He picks up a script and reads.*) 'The Story of a Horse and the Horse Who Loved Him.' (*He drops script.*) ... Give me a breather from all those fine folk suddenly see what a great 'man' I am. N'when I *do* return my calls, Charl, do you know what I'll tell those people?

Fox No.

Gould I'm going to tell them 'Go through Channels.' This protects me from them. And from folk, fine as they are, like you, Charl, when you come to me for favors. Or did you come up here to congratulate me on my new promotion?

Fox Congratulations.

Gould Do I deserve it?

Fox Yes. You do, Bob.

Gould Why?

Fox Because you're a prince among men and you're Yertle the Turtle.

Gould Alright then, that's enough. What did you bring me?

Fox This morning, Bob.

Gould Yes?

Fox This morning Doug Brown came to me.

Gould . . . Doug Brown.

Fox (*pause*) He came to my *house* Bob. How would you *like* . . . How would you like for Doug Brown to 'cross the street' to do a picture for us? (*Pause.*) Bob? How would you *like*, a script that I got him. He's *nuts* for it, he's free, we could start to shoot next *month*, I have his word and he'll come to the studio, and do the film for us. Doug Brown will cross the street and do a film for us next month.

Gould (*picks up phone*) Get me Ross. (*Pause.*)

Fox . . . do you see what I'm telling you?

Gould . . . he came to your house . . .

Fox . . . can you believe what I'm saying to you . . . ?

Gould Douggie Brown. (*Into phone.*) Ross (*Pause.*) *Richard Ross* . . . no, no, no, *don't* look in the book . . . there's a button on the console . . . Richard R . . . just push the button on the . . . (*Pause.*) There's a button on the console . . . Richard Ross . . . just . . . *Thank* you. (*Hangs up the phone. Pause.*) Are you alright?

Fox I'm fine. I'm fine, I just need coffee.

Gould We'll get it for you. Tell mmm . . .

Fox Alright, I, this is some time ago.

Gould ...uh huh...

Fox That I get the script to Brown...

Gould What script...?

Fox You don't know it, a prison script...

Gould (*simultaneously with 'script'*) One of ours...?

Fox I found it in the file. I *loved* it... all the time I'm thinking...

Gould Uh huh...

Fox How to do this script, I, one day...

Gould Uh huh...

Fox ...so...

Gould So, you give the script to Brown...

Fox Not 'him', his...

Gould Uh huh...

Fox ...his...

Gould ...I know...

Fox His 'guy'.

Gould Yes.

Fox *Gives* Douggie the script...

Phone rings. **Gould** *picks up the phone.*

Gould (*into phone*) Yes. Thank you. (*Hangs up.*) Ross'll get back to us...

Fox ...His guy *gives* Douggie the scri...

Gould He gives Douggie the script.

Fox Yes.

Gould Mmm...

Fox *Months* ago, alright? *I* don't know. *Today*, alright...? Today. (*Pause.*) I'm having coffee...

Gould Umm hmmm...

Fox Who drives up?

Gould ...coffee at your house...

Fox Who drives up?

Gould Douggie Brown.

Fox Douglas Brown drives up to my house. (*Pause.*) He says 'I Want To Do Your Script. I've got this other thing to deal with, and we'll settle it tomorrow. Call me ten o'clock tomorrow morning. I'll come in and sign *up*.' (*Phone rings.*)

Gould (*into phone*) *Hello*...who? No calls. *No* calls. Just Richard Ross. And we need coffee...okay? *Got* it...? (*Hangs up.*)

Fox ...cross the street to shoot it...? And he says 'why not'. (*Pause.*)

Gould ...*huh*...

Fox *Huh*...?

Gould ...He'd come over here to shoot it...

Fox Sonofabitch like out of some damn fairytale.

Gould ...he drove to your house...

Fox ...I'm looking out the window...

Gould ...son of a bitch...

Fox ...Douglas Brown drives up...

The phone rings. **Gould** *picks it up.*

Gould (*into phone*) Hello. Yes. *Richard*... (*Pause.*) Yes. Put him...Hello, *Richard*. Fine, just fine. They're painting it. Well, thank you. Thank you. Listen Richard. Do you need some good news...? (*Pause.*) Well, it's a surprise that I've got for you. No, I want to tell you in person. Do you have five mi...(*Checks watch.*) We'll be there. (*Pause.*) Charlie Fox... *Charlie* came in with a...(*Pause.*) Right. Right. We'll be there. Right. (*Hangs up.*) Well. We see him in ten minutes.

Fox *Yessir.* I need some coffee.

Gould Oh, Jesus, what's the...

Fox What...?

Gould The, what's the story? Tell me the . . .

Fox *I* can tell it. No, you're right. *You* tell it.

Gould Gimme the broad outl . . .

Fox Yes, yes.

Gould Just sketch me the broad . . .

Fox Yes, yes, the *thing*, of course, is . . .

Gould Douggie, Brown, of course, the thing . . .

Fox 'A Douggie Brown picture' . . .

Gould A Douggie Brown picture . . .

Fox Eh? A buddy . . .

Gould A *Buddy* Picture.

Fox Douggie and . . .

Gould 'Watch this space', I got it . . .

Fox Right.

Gould The Flavor of the Month . . . okay, now, what's the story?

Fox Doug's in prison.

Gould . . . prison . . .

Fox Right. These guys, they want to get him.

Gould *Black* guys . . .

Fox Black guys in the prison.

Gould (*into phone*) Coffee, quickly, can you get some coffee in here? (*Hangs up.*)

Fox And the black guys going to rape his ass.

Gould Mmm.

Fox Okay. Now. 'Now, you could,' he goes, 'you could have "your way" with me, all of you . . . '

Gould Uh huh, what? ten or twenty guys . . .

Fox ' . . . and you could *do* that. But I'd have to, you see? Here's the *thing* of it. Unless you *killed* me, I would . . . '

Gould Uh huh . . .

Fox ' . . . have to come back and *retaliate*, sometime, somehow, because . . .'

Gould . . . okay . . .

Fox 'I couldn't . . .'

Gould . . . uh huh . . .

Fox ' . . . *live* with that.'

Gould . . . The degradation . . .

Fox 'So whyn't you skip all the *middle* shit, kill me right now.'

Gould . . . he throws it in their face.

Fox You got it.

Gould . . . uh huh . . .

Fox '*Or*.' (*Pause*.) Or . . .

Gould . . . yes . . .

Fox 'If you could use a *friend*, why not allow me this? To *be* your friend . . .'

Gould He teams up with the guys . . .

Fox 'To *side* with you . . .'

Gould Yes.

Fox 'and *together* . . .'

Gould . . . and . . .

Fox . . . they become friends, they teach him the . . .

Gould . . . he learns the Prison Ways . . .

Fox They blah blah, *so* on . . .

Gould Uh huh . . .

Fox *Now*. Eh? Now. With his, his knowledge of *computers*, so on, with his *money* . . .

Gould . . . yeah . . .

Fox His Links to the Outside . . .

Gould A girl . . . ?

Fox Ah. Now that's the *great* part, I'm telling you, when I saw this script . . .

Gould . . . I don't know how it got past us . . .

Fox When they get out of *prison*, the Head Convict's Sister . . .

Gould . . . a buddy film, a prison film, Douggie Brown, blah, blah, some girl . . .

Fox Action, a social . . .

Gould Action, blood, a social theme . . .

Fox (*simultaneously with 'theme'*) That's what I'm *saying*, an offbeat . . .

Gould Good. Good. Good. Alright. Now: Now: when we go in . . .

Fox That's what I'm saying. Bob.

Gould Don't even say it.

Fox Bob:

Gould I understand.

Fox . . . I wanted to say . . .

Gould I know what you wanted to say, and you're right. I know what you're going to ask, and I'm going to see you get it. Absolutely right: You go on this package as the co-producer. (*Pause.*) The name above the title. This is your . . .

Fox . . . thank you . . .

Gould *Thank* me?

Fox Thank you, Bob.

Gould *Hey*: You came in here.

Fox . . . thank you . . .

Gould Hey, Charl, it's *right* . . .

Fox No, but the thing is that you *thought* of it. You thought of me. You thought to *say* it.

Gould I should be thanking you and I *do* thank you.

Fox Thank you, Bob.

Gould This is your thing and you should get a bump.

Fox Thank you.

Gould Because. *Charlie*: Don't thank me. You start me off here with a bang. I know that you could have Gone Across the Street . . .

Fox I wouldn't have done that.

Gould But you could.

Fox I wouldn't . . .

Gould But you *could*. And that's the point, Charl. That you absolutely *could*. And it was 'loyalty' kept you with us . . .

Fox Hey, hey, it's only common sense.

Gould You stuck with the Home Store.

Fox Hey, you've been good for me, to put it bluntly, all the years . . .

Gould . . . you stuck with the Old Firm, Charl, you stuck with your friends.

Fox It's where I work, Bob, it's what I *do*, and my relationship with you . . . we were all happy for you, Bob, you got bumped up, and I feel that I'm lucky . . .

Gould *I'm* the lucky one, Charl . . .

Fox Hey, Bullshit, to have somebody I could *come* to . . .

Gould (*simultaneously with 'come'*) Because you *could* have gone Across the Street. Who would have blamed you?

Fox Yeah, but I wouldn't of done it.

Gould Who would of blamed you, Charl? You get a Free Option on a Douggie Brown film, guys would walk in here, hold a guy up . . .

Fox I work here, Bob. And my loyalty has always been to you. (*Pause.*)

Gould Well, I'm one lucky son of a bitch . . .

Fox That you are.

Gould And what I do is 'owe you'.

Fox No, no, Bob. Bull*shit* . . . The times you've . . .

Gould I'm just doing my job.

Fox No, I know, I know . . . and I know at times, that it was *difficult* for you . . .

Gould No.

Fox I, and I hesitate to *ask* it, to ask for the credit . . .

Gould . . . Don't *have* to ask it.

Fox 'Cause I know, anybody was to *come* in here, *exploit* you . . . this thing . . .

Gould . . . *Forget* . . .

Fox . . . your new 'position', all, I even hesitate . . .

Gould Don't hesitate about a goddamn thing, *forget* it, Charl: *You Brought Me Gold.* You're gonna be co-producer. What the fuck are you *talkin'* about . . . ?

Fox I just, I wanted to say . . .

Gould (*simultaneously with 'say'*) I'm grateful to *you*, pal. For *this* n'for all that you've been, over the years . . .

Fox Now . . . *you* know . . .

Gould Hey, hey, hey. (**Gould** *checks his watch.*) Let's go make some money. (*He rises.*)

Fox I, I need a cuppa coffee . . .

Gould You get it in Ross's office. Here's how we play it: we get *in* . . .

Fox . . . yes . . .

Gould We get in, get out and we give it to him *in one sentence.* Let *me* talk, no disrespect . . .

Fox No.

Gould But it's courtesy . . .

Fox I understand.

Gould One sentence. 'Doug Brown, Buddy Film.' (*Phone rings. Into phone.*) Whoever it is, we'll be with Mr Rrr . . . (*Pause.*) Yes? Put him on . . . Hello: *Richard* . . . Yes . . . ? Yes,

well, how long will you bbb . . . (*Pause.*) I see . . . Absolutely.
(*Pause.*) No problem whatsoever . . . you'll be *back* by
then . . . ? (*Pause.*) Absolutely so. Thank you. (*He hangs up.
Pause. To* **Fox**.) Ross just got called to New York. He's going
on the Gulfstream, turn around and come right back. So we
got pushed to tomorrow morning, ten o'clock.

Fox (*pause*) *Aha.* (*Pause.*)

Gould No help for it.

Fox I've got, Douggie only gave me until . . .

Gould . . . I'm sorry . . .

Fox Doug Brown only gave me until ten tomorrow morn . . .

Gould No, I know, we've only got 'til ten to tie . . .

Fox We got to come up with a Pay or Play to *tie* him to this
thing by ten o'clock to . . .

Gould No problem. Ross'll be back for tomorrow morning,
if he *doesn't* . . .

Fox . . . if he doesn't . . .

Gould . . . yes . . .

Fox . . . then . . .

Gould . . . Then we'll raise him on the *phone* . . .

Fox . . . I'm saying . . .

Gould Wherever he is, we'll pull him *out* of *it* . . .

Fox Wherever he is.

Gould Yup.

Fox Because I only got the option until ten o'clock
tomorrow. Doug Brown told me . . .

Gould Yeah. I'm *saying*. Ten o'clock tomorrow. Ross: he'll
be here, one chance in a *quillion* he isn't, then we go Condition
Red, we get him on the . . .

Fox . . . because . . .

Gould Yeah, yeah, yeah, I'm *with* you.

Fox Be . . .

Gould ... You understand ... I wanted to do ...

Fox ... I understand ...

Gould I wanted to do it in *person* ...

Fox Yes.

Gould ... 'Cause you're gonna be the Bringer of Good *News* ...

Fox No, no, you're absolutely right.

Gould Do it in *person* ...

Fox ... yes ...

Gould And forge that bond.

Fox It's just ...

Gould Don't worry.

Fox Not me. It's just, you move up to *the big league* ... (*Pause.*)

Gould Charlie. Your ship has come in ...

Fox (*pause*) ... all I'm saying ... *Ross* ...

Gould What's Ross going to say ... 'No'? It's *done*.

Fox Lord, I believe, aid thou my unbelief ... the sucker walked in, said 'I love the script.'

Gould Oh yes, Charlie, for we're now the *Fair*-haired boys.

Fox I couldn't believe it, you talk, talk about, talk, what is the ... 'watersheds'.

Gould That's right.

Fox And, that is one of them.

Gould And why *shouldn't* it be – you understand ... ?

Fox *I* don't know.

Gould 'Cause you ...

Fox ... I, I don't know ...

Gould ... You *worked* for it ... you know, you know ...

Fox 'I'm going to be rich and I can't believe it.'

Gould Rich, are you kidding me? We're going to have to hire someone just to figure out the *things* we want to buy . . .

Fox I mean, I mean, you think about a concept, all your life . . .

Gould . . . I'm with you . . .

Fox 'Wealth.'

Gould Yes. Wealth.

Fox Then it comes *down* to you . . .

Gould Uh huh . . .

Fox All you can think of . . . '*This* is what that means . . .'

Gould And that *is* what it means. (*Pause.*)

Fox How, how, figuring up the rentals, tie in, foreign, air, the . . .

Gould Uh, huh . . .

Fox Over the course . . .

Gould . . . don't forget the sequels.

Fox Do we . . . we're tied in to that . . . ?

Gould Are we tied in to that, Charl? Welcome to the world.

Fox Hhhhh. How . . . (*Pause.*)

Gould The question, your crass question: how much money could we stand to make . . . ?

Fox Yes.

Gould I think the operative concept here is 'lots and lots . . .'

Fox Oh, maan . . .

Gould Great big jolly *shitloads* of it.

Fox Oh, maan . . .

Gould But money . . .

Fox Yeah.

Gould Money, Charl . . .

Fox Yeah . . .

Gould Money is not the important thing.

Fox No.

Gould Money is not Gold.

Fox No.

Gould What can you do with Money?

Fox Nothing.

Gould Nary a goddamn thing.

Fox ... I'm gonna be rich.

Gould 'Buy' things with it.

Fox Where would I *keep* them?

Gould What would you *do* with them?

Fox Yeah.

Gould Take them out and *dust* them, time to time.

Fox Oh yeah.

Gould I piss on money.

Fox I know that you do. I'll help you.

Gould *Fuck* money.

Fox Fuck it. Fuck 'things' too ...

Gould Uh huh. But don't fuck 'people'.

Fox No.

Gould 'Cause, people, Charlie ...

Fox People ... yes.

Gould Are what it's All About.

Fox I know.

Gould And it's a People Business.

Fox That it is.

Gould It's *full* of fucken' people ...

Fox And we're gonna kick some ass, Bob.

Gould That we are.

Fox We're gonna kick the ass of a lot of them fucken' people.

Gould That's right.

Fox We get rolling, Bob. It's 'up the ass with gun and camera'.

Gould Yup.

Fox 'Cause when you spend twenty years in the barrel . . .

Gould . . . I know . . .

Fox No, you *don't* know, you've forgotten. Due respect.

Gould . . . may be . . .

Fox But, but . . . oh maan . . . I'm gonna settle some fucken' scores.

Gould Better things to do . . .

Fox If there are, *show* them to me, man . . . A bunch of cocksuckers out there. Gimme' a cigarette. Oh, Man, I can't come down.

Gould No need to. Huh . . . ?

Fox Ross, Ross, Ross isn't going to fuck me out of this . . . ?

Gould No. Absolutely not. You have my word.

Fox I don't need your word, Bob. I know *you* . . . Drives right to my house. I need a cup of coffee.

Gould (*into phone*) Could we get a cup . . . well, where did you try? Why not try the *coffee mach* . . . well, it's right down at the . . . down the, no, it's unmarked, just go . . . that's right. (*Hangs up.*)

Fox What, you got a new broad, go with the new job . . .

Gould No. Cathy's just out sick.

Fox Cute broad, the new broad.

Gould What? She's cute? The broad out there is cute? Baby, she's nothing. You wait 'til we make this film.

Fox She's nothing?

Gould Playing in this league? I'm saying, it's Boy's Choice: Skate in One Direction Only. (*Pause.*)

Fox Oh, man, what am I going to *do* today?

Gould Go to a movie, get your hair done.

Fox I'm jumping like a leaf.

Gould It's a done deal. We walk in *tomorrow* . . .

Fox (*picks up the book*) What's this, what's the thing you're reading I come in?

Gould This thing?

Fox Uh huh . . .

Gould From the East. An Eastern Sissy Writer. (*Passes the book to* **Fox**.)

Fox (*reads*) 'The Bridge: or, Radiation and the Half-Life of Society. A Study of Decay.'

Gould A Novel.

Fox Great.

Gould A cover note from Richard Ross: 'Give this a Courtesy Read.'

Fox (*reads*) 'The wind against the Plains, but not a wind of change . . . a wind like that one which he'd been foretold, the rubbish of the world – swirling, swirling . . . two thousand years . . .' Hey I wouldn't just give it a *courtesy* read, I'd *make* this sucker.

Gould Good idea.

Fox Drop a dime on western civilization.

Gould . . . 'Bout time.

Fox Why don't you do that? *Make* it.

Gould I think that I will.

Fox Yeah. Instead of our Doug, Doug Brown's *Buddy* film.

Gould Yeah. *I* could do that. You know why? Because my job, my new job is one thing: the capacity to make decisions.

Fox I know that it is.

Gould Decide, decide, decide . . .

Fox It's lonely at the top.

Gould But it ain't crowded.

Karen, *the secretary, comes in with a tray of coffee.*

Karen I'm sorry, please, but how do you take your coffee . . . ?

Fox He takes his coffee like he makes his movies: nothing in it.

Gould Very funny.

Fox 'Cause he's an Old Whore.

Gould . . . that's right . . .

Fox Bobby Gould . . .

Gould . . . Huh . . .

Fox You're just an Old Whore.

Gould Proud of it. Yes, yes.

Fox They kick you upstairs and you're still just some old whore.

Gould You're an old whore, too.

Fox I never said I wasn't. Soon to be a *rich* old whore.

Gould That's right.

Fox And I deserve it.

Gould That you do, Babe, that you do.

Fox Because, Miss, lemme tell you something, I've been *loyal* to this guy, you know, you know . . . *what's* your name?

Karen Karen . . .

Fox Karen, lemme tell you: since the *mail* room . . . you know? Step-by-step. Yes, in his shadow, yes, why not. Never forgot him, and he never forgot me.

Gould That's absolutely right.

Fox You know why I never forgot him?

Karen . . . I . . .

Fox . . . Because the shit of his I had to eat, how *could* I forget him?

Gould . . . huh . . .

Fox Yes, but the Wheel Came Around. And here we are. Two Whores. (*To* **Gould**.) You're gonna decorate your office. Make it a bordello. You'll feel more at home.

Gould *You*, you sonofabitch . . .

Fox . . . and come to work in a soiled nightgown.

Gould Hey, after the Doug Brown thing, I come to work in that same nightgown, I say 'kiss the hem', then every swinging dick in this man's studio will kiss that hem.

Fox They will.

Gould They'll *french* that jolly jolly hem.

Fox Uh huh, uh huh . . . *you*, you, you fucken' whore, on his deathbed, St Peter'll come for him, his dying words, 'Just let me turn One More Trick . . . '

Gould I'm a whore and I'm proud of it. But I'm a *secure* whore. Yes, and you get *ready*, now: you get ready 'cause they're going to plot, they're going to plot against you . . . (*To* **Karen**.) Karen. My friend's stepping up in class . . . (*To* **Fox**.) They're going to plot against you, Charlie, like they plotted against me. They're going to go back in their Tribal Caves and say 'Chuck Fox, that *hack* . . . '

Fox 'That powerful hack . . . '

Gould Let's go and steal his job . . .

Karen Sir . . . ?

Fox Black, two sugars, thank you.

Gould To your face they'll go, 'Three bags full.' And behind your back they'll say, 'let's tear him down – let's tear Charlie Fox down . . . '

Fox Behind my back. Yes, but in Public . . . ? They'll say: 'I waxed Mr Fox's car. He seemed pleased.'

Karen (*serving coffee*) Black, two sugars.

Fox 'I blew his poodle. He gave me a smile.' (*Of coffee.*) Thank you.

Gould This is Charlie Fox. This is . . . *Karen* . . .

Fox Yes. Good morning.

Karen Good morning, sir.

Gould Please put me down. Tomorrow. Richard Ross. His office. Ten a.m. Whatever you find in the book, call back and *cancel* it. And leave a note for Cathy, should she be back . . .

Karen I'm told that she'll be back tomorrow.

Gould . . . draw her attention to our meeting with Ross.

Karen Yessir.

Fox Karen, as Mr Gould moves on up the ladder, will you go with him?

Karen Sir?

Fox When . . .

Karen I'm just a temporary . . .

Gould That's right, she's just here for a . . .

Fox Well, would you like stay on, if . . .

Gould Hey, what are you? The Master of the Revels?

Karen I'm just, I'm on a temporary . . .

Fox Hey, everything's temporary 'til it's 'not' . . .

Karen No, this is just a temporary job.

Gould It's just a temporary job – so leave the girl alone.

Fox Karen: yeah: Karen, this seem like a good place to work?

Karen Sir?

Fox Call me Charlie. This seem like a good place to work?

Karen Here?

Fox Mr Gould's office.

Karen I'm sure that it is.

Fox She's 'sure that it is'. How wonderful to be so sure. How wonderful to have such certainty in this wonderful world. Hey, Bobby . . . ? Your boss tells you 'take initiative', you best guess right – and you *do*, then you get no credit. Day-in, . . . smiling, smiling, just a cog.

Gould Mr Fox is taking about his own self.

Fox You *bet* I am. But my historical self, Bob, for I am a cog no more.

Gould Karen, you come here at an auspicious time.

Fox *Give* this man a witness.

Gould Because in this sinkhole of slime and depravity, something is about to work out.

Fox . . . singing a song, rolling along.

Gould . . . and all that garbage that we put up with is going to pay off. (*Pause.*)

Karen . . . why is it garbage . . . ? (*Pause.*)

Gould It's not all garbage, but most of it is.

Karen Why?

Gould Why. That's a good . . . (*To* **Fox**.) Why? (*Pause.*)

Fox Because.

Gould (*to* **Karen**) Because.

Fox Life in the movie business is like the, is like the beginning of a new love affair: it's full of surprises, and you're constantly getting fucked.

Karen But why should it all be garbage?

Fox Why? Why should nickels be bigger than dimes? That's the way it is.

Gould It's a business, with its own unchanging rules. Isn't that right, Charlie?

Fox Yes, it is. The *one* thing is: nobody pays off on work.

Gould That is the truth.

Fox Everybody says 'Hey, I'm a maverick.'

Gould That's it . . .

Fox But what do they do? Sit around like, hey, Pancho-the-dead-whale . . .

Gould ...huh...

Fox Waiting for the...

Gould ...mmm...

Fox Yeah...? The Endorsement of their Superiors...

Gould Uh huh. Listen to the guy. He's telling you.

Fox You wanna *do* something out here, it better be one of The Five Major Food Groups.

Gould Uh huh.

Fox Or your superiors go napsy – bye. The *upside* of which, though, a guy...

Gould ...that's right...

Fox The *upside*...

Gould Hmm.

Fox The *upside*, though...

Gould ...Hmm.

Fox The one time you *do* get support...

Gould ...hey...

Fox If you *do* have a relationship...

Gould Hey, Charl, kidding aside, that is what I'm here for...

Fox Then, you can do something. (*To* **Karen**, *of* **Gould**.) This guy, Karen, this guy... the last eleven years.

Gould *Forget* it...

Fox Forget? Bullshit. This man, my friend...

Gould Now we're even.

Fox Oh, you Beauty... What's it like being Head of Production? I mean, is it more fun than miniature golf?

Gould You put as much energy in your job as you put into kissing my ass...

Fox My job *is* kissing your ass.

Gould And don't you forget it.

Fox Not a chance. (*Pause.*)

Karen Sir:

Gould Yes.

Karen (*pause*) I feel silly saying it.

Gould What?

Karen I ...

Gould Well, whatever it is, say it.

Karen (*pause*) I don't know what to do. (*Pause.*) I don't know what I'm supposed to do. (*Pause.*)

Gould Well, that was very frank of you. I tell you what: don't do anything.

Karen Sir ... ?

Gould We'll call it a Bank Holiday. (*To* **Fox**.) Huh? Let's get out of here.

Fox Good, let's get out of here.

Gould Huh?

Fox Well done.

Gould And let's get out of here. (*To* **Karen**.) Look in my book, and *cancel* whatever I've got today. Anybody calls, call me tomorrow. I'll be in tomorrow for my ten a.m. meeting with Ross.

Fox Young America at WORK and PLAY.

Gould You get done cancelling my stuff, you can go home.

Fox Where we going for lunch?

Gould Well, I figured we'd drop by the commissary, get the tuna sandwich, then go swishing by Laura Ashley and pick out some cunning prints for my new office.

Fox Whyn't you just paint it with broken capillaries, decorate it like the inside of your nose.

Gould I may. I just may. So, lunch, the Coventry, in half an hour. (*To* **Karen**.) Call the Coventry. Table for two, at One.

Thank you. (*She exits. Pause. He sighs.*) First in war. First in peace. First in the hearts of Pee Wee Reese.

Fox   Lunch at the Coventry.

Gould   That's right.

Fox   Thy will be done.

Gould   You see, all that you got to do is eat my doo doo for eleven years, and eventually the wheel comes round.

Fox   Pay back time.

Gould   You brought me the Doug Brown script.

Fox   Glad I could do it.

Gould   You son of a *bitch* . . .

Fox   Hey.

Gould   Charl, I just hope.

Fox   What?

Gould   The shoe was on the other foot, I'd act in such a . . .

Fox   . . . hey . . .

Gould   Really, princely way toward *you*.

Fox   I *know* you would, Bob, because lemme tell you: experiences like this, *films* like this . . . these are the films . . .

Gould   . . . Yes . . .

Fox   *These* are the films, that whaddayacallit . . . (*Long pause.*) that make it all worthwhile.

Gould   . . . I think you're going to find a *lot* of things now, make it all worthwhile. I think *conservatively*, you and me, we build ourselves in to split, minimally, ten percent. (*Pause.*)

Fox   Of the net.

Gould   Char, Charlie: permit me to tell you: two things I've learned, twenty-five years in the entertainment industry.

Fox   What?

Gould   The two things which are always true.

Fox   One:

Gould The first one is: there is no net.

Fox Yeah . . . ? (*Pause.*)

Gould And I forgot the second one. Okay, I'm gonna meet you at the Coventry in half an hour. We'll talk about boys and clothes.

Fox Whaddaya gonna do the interim?

Gould I'm gonna *Work* . . . (*Indicating his figures on the pad.*)

Fox Work . . . ? You never did a day's work in your life.

Gould Oooh, Oooh, . . . the Bitching Lamp is Lit.

Fox You never did a fucken' day's work in your life.

Gould That true?

Fox Eleven years I've known you, you're either scheming or you're ziggin' and zaggin', hey, I *know* you, Bob.

Gould Oh yes, the scorn of the impotent . . .

Fox I know you, Bob. I know you from the *back*. *I* know what you're staying for.

Gould You do?

Fox Yes.

Gould What?

Fox You're staying to Hide the Afikomen.

Gould Yeah?

Fox You're staying to put those moves on your new secretary.

Gould I am?

Fox Yeah, and it *will* not work.

Gould It will not work, what are you saying . . . ?

Fox No, I was just saying that she . . .

Gould . . . she wouldn't go for me.

Fox That she won't go for you.

Gould (*pause*) Why?

Fox Why? (*Pause.*) *I* don't know.

Gould What do you see . . . ?

Fox I think . . . I think . . . you serious?

Gould Yes.

Fox I don't want to pee on your parade.

Gould No . . .

Fox I mean, I'm sorry that I took the edge off it.

Gould I wasn't *going* to hit on her.

Fox Hmmm.

Gould I was gonna . . .

Fox You were gonna work.

Gould Yes.

Fox Oh.

Gould (*pause*) But tell me what you see.

Fox What I see, what I *saw*, just an observation . . .

Gould . . . yes . . .

Fox It's not important.

Gould Tell me what you see. Really.

Fox I just thought, I just thought she falls between two stools.

Gould And what would those stools be?

Fox That she is not, just some, you know, a 'floozy' . . .

Gould A 'floozy' . . .

Fox . . . on the other hand, I think I'd have to say, I don't think she is so *ambitious* she would schtup you just to get ahead. (*Pause.*) That's all. (*Pause.*)

Gould What if she just 'liked' me? (*Pause.*)

Fox If she just 'liked' you?

Gould Yes.

Fox Ummm. (*Pause.*)

Gould Yes.

Fox You're saying, if she just . . . *liked* you . . . (*Pause.*)

Gould You mean nobody loves me for myself.

Fox No.

Gould No?

Fox Not in *this* office . . .

Gould And she's neither, what, vacant nor ambitious enough to go . . .

Fox . . . I'm not saying you don't *deserve* it, you *do* deserve it. Hey, . . . I think you're worth it.

Gould Thank you. You're saying that she's neither, what, dumb, nor ambitious enough, she would go to bed with me.

Fox . . . she's too, she's too . . .

Gould She's too . . . High-line . . . ?

Fox No, she's, she's too . . .

Gould She's too . . .

Fox . . . yes.

Gould Then what's she doing in this office?

Fox She's a *Temporary* Worker.

Gould You're full of it, Chuck.

Fox Maybe. And I didn't mean to take the *shine* off our . . .

Gould Hey, hey, he sends the cross, he sends the strength to bear it. Go to, go to lunch, I'll meet you at . . .

Fox I didn't mean to imply . . .

Gould Imply. Naaa. Nobody Loves Me. Nobody loves me for myself. Hey, Big Deal, don't go mopin' on me here. We'll go and celebrate. A Douglas Brown Film. Fox and Gould . . .

Fox . . . you're very kind . . .

Gould . . . you brought the guy in. Fox and Gould Present:

Fox I'll see you at lunch . . . (*Starts to exit.*)

Gould But I bet she would go, I bet she *would* go out with me.

Fox I bet she would, too.

Gould No, No. I'm saying, I think that she 'likes' me.

Fox Yeah. I'm sure she does.

Gould No, joking apart, Babe. My *perceptions* . . . Say I'm nuts, I don't *think* so – she likes me, and she'd go out with me.

Fox How much?

Gould How much? Seriously . . . ? (*Pause.*)

Fox Yeah.

Gould . . . that she would . . . ?

Fox Yeah. That she would *anything*. (*Pause.*) That she would anything. (*Pause.*) That she would deal with you in any other than a professional way. (*Pause.*)

Gould Well, my, my, my, my, my.

Fox What can I tell you, '*Bob*'.

Gould That I can get her on a date, that I can get her to my house, that I can screw her.

Fox I don't think so.

Gould How much? (*Pause.*)

Fox A hundred bucks.

Gould That's enough?

Fox Five hundred bucks that you can't.

Gould Five hundred? That's enough?

Fox A gentleman's bet.

Gould Done. Now get out of here, and let me work . . . the Coventry at One. I need . . .

Fox The script, the budget, chain of ownership . . .

Gould Good.

Fox I'll swing by my, I'll bring it to lunch.

Gould Good. Char . . . (*Pause.*)

Fox What?

Gould Thank you.

Fox Hey. Fuck you. (*Exits.*)

Gould *sits alone for a moment, writing.* **Karen** *enters.*

Karen Mr Gould . . .

Gould Bobby.

Karen Sir. (*Pause.*) I was not able to get you a table at the Coventry. But I tentatively booked you at . . .

Gould Whoa, whoa, whoa, whoa. (*Pause.*) It's alright. I'm going to tell you what you did, and it's alright you did it. Sit down. You called up the Coventry and asked them for a table for two at one o'clock. And they told you they had absolutely nothing. That right?

Karen Yes. (*Pause.*) I . . . I . . . I'm so sorry. Of course. I should have mentioned your name.

Gould It's alright.

Karen It was very . . . it was *naïve* of me.

Gould It's alright.

Karen I had . . . no: you're right. I had a thought, when I was hanging up, then I thought: 'You forgot to . . .'

Gould . . . it's alright.

Karen 'You forgot to "tell" them,' then I thought: 'what difference does it make? If they don't have a *table* . . .'

Gould It's alright.

Karen If they didn't have a table, what difference who called up? But, of *course*, they have a table for *you* . . . I'm sorry. It was naïve of me.

Gould Listen, there's nothing wrong with being naïve, with learning . . .

Karen (*simultaneously with 'learning'*) And I'm sure . . . I'm sorry.

Gould No, go on.

Karen . . . I was going to say . . .

Gould . . . yes . . . ?

Karen I was going to say that I'm sure that much of a job like this, a job like this, is learning to think in a . . .

Gould Yes.

Karen To think in a . . . business fashion.

Gould That's what makes the life exciting, *addictive*, *you* know what I'm talking about, you want a *thrill* in your life?

Karen . . . a thrill . . . ?

Gould To *make* something, to *do* something, to be a *part* of something. Money, art, a chance to Play at the Big Table . . . Hey, you're here, and you want to participate in it. (*Pause.*)

Karen Yes.

Gould Well, of course you do. And it *is* an exciting world.

Karen I'm sure it is.

Gould Sudden changes all the time. You want to *know* some of it. Now, you want to know a secret?

Karen Yes.

Gould I'll *tell* you one. Siddown. (**Karen** *sits.*) Charlie Fox comes in and he's formed a relationship with Doug Brown. Doug will leave his studio and do a film with us. Charlie Fox brought it to us, brought it to *me* really. And in the Highest Traditions of the Motion Picture Industry, we're actually going to make a movie.

Karen Is it a good film?

Gould I'm sorry.

Karen Is it a good film?

Gould Well, it's a commodity. And I admire you for not being ashamed to ask the question. Yes, it's a good question, and I don't *know* if it is a good film. 'What about Art?' I'm not an artist. Never said I was, and nobody who sits in this chair can be. I'm a businessman. 'Can't we try to make good films?' Yes. We try. I'm going to try to make a good film of this prison film. The question: Is there such a thing as a good film which loses money? In general, of course. But, really, not. For *me*, 'cause if the films I make lose money, then I'm back on the streets with a sweet and silly smile on my face, they lost money 'cause nobody saw them, it's my fault. A tree fell in the forest, what did I accomplish? Yes. You *see*? There is a way things are. Some people are elected, try to change the world, this job is not that job. Somebody, somebody . . . in this job, in the job I have, somebody is always trying to 'promote' you: to use *something*, some 'hook' to get you to do something in their own best interest. You follow me?

Karen Of course.

Gould 'Cause this *desk* is a position to *advance*, y'understand? It's a *platform* to *aid*, to push someone along. But I Can't *Do* It. Why? That's not my business. My business is to make decisions for the studio. Means I have to be *blunt*, to say 'no', much, most of the time, that's my job. And I think it's a *good* job: 'cause it's a job of *responsibility*. Pressure, many rewards. *One* of them, one time in a billion years, someone was loyal to me, and I'm talking about Charlie Fox, stuck *with* me, comes in here, let's face it, does a favor for me . . . he could of took the script across the street, no, but he came to me, now – I can throw in with him and we rise together. That's what the job is. It's a job, all the bullshit aside, deals with *people*. (*He hunts on his desk, picks up a copy of the book he was reading from earlier.*) Look here. Agent gives his client's book to Ross: 'The Bridge or, Radiation and the Half-Life of Society': Now, *who* is Mister Ross, now . . . ?

Karen He is the Head of the Studio.

Gould And he has a button on my console. That's right. Author's agent gave this book to Ross. A novel. Written by a Very Famous Eastern Writer. What's this book about? 'The End of the World.' Great. Now: Ross, no dummy, says, of course, he'll read the book. Gives *me* the book to read, so when he tells the author 'how he loved the book but it won't make a movie,' he can say something intelligent about it. You get it? This, in the business, is called 'a courtesy read'.

Karen A courtesy read.

Gould Yes. No one has any intention of making the book, but we read it, as a courtesy. Does this mean that we're depraved? No. It's just business . . . how business is done, you see?

Karen I think.

Gould A business. Start to close.

Karen But what if there is something in the book?

Gould In the book?

Karen Yes. (*Pause.*)

Gould It's a novel about the historical effects of radiation . . .

Karen Yes, but . . .

Gould I mean, I mean, the author's crazy as a fucken' June bug.

Karen But, but.

Gould . . . what if . . . ?

Karen Yes.

Gould What if, after everything . . .

Karen Yes.

Gould Hope against hope, there is *something* in the book.

Karen Yes.

Gould *Something* in the book, that . . .

Karen Yes. (*Pause.*)

Gould Well, I'd be delighted. No. You're right. You're right. I'll tell you. (*Pause.*) You're making my point. Absolutely. This job corrupts you. You start to think, all the time 'what do these people want from me?' (*Pause.*) And everything becomes a task. (*Pause.*)

Karen Does it have to be that?

Gould Can we keep ourselves pure? Hey, I prayed to be pure.

Karen You prayed? To be pure?

Gould I did, I said God give me the job as Head of Production. Give me a platform to be 'good', and I'll be good. They gave me the job, I'm here one day and *look* at me: a Big Fat Whore. A book, it may be a *fine, fine* book by a well-respected writer. And because this writer's got the reputation

being 'artsy' . . . artsy, you understand . . . I'm ready,
everybody backs me up in this, to assume that his book is
unsuitable for the screen, so I look on it as a 'courtesy read'.

Karen Do you enjoy your work?

Gould Excuse me?

Karen Do, if I'm being too frank . . .

Gould . . . do I enjoy my work? Yes. Very much. (*Pause.*)
Don't you think *you* would enjoy it?

Karen Yes, I think I would enjoy it.

Gould You do? Good for you. What of it would you enjoy?

Karen The making decisions.

Gould Then good for you.

Karen Because . . .

Gould . . . yes . . . ?

Karen Perhaps I'm naïve, but I would think that if you
could keep your values straight, if you had *principles* to *refer* to,
then . . .

Gould Hmmm.

Karen I know it's naïve . . .

Gould Yes it is naïve, and it's also correct.

Karen You think it is?

Gould Yes, I do. Now, we could talk about purity or we
could turn the page. What do you want to do?

Karen Talk about purity.

Gould Okay. (*Pause.*) If you don't have *principles*, whatever
they are . . . then each day is hell, you haven't got a compass.
All you've got is 'good taste'; and you can shove good taste up
your ass and fart 'The Carnival of Venice'. Good taste will not
hack it. 'Cause each day the pressure just gets worse. It gets
more difficult. (*Pause.*) I want you to do me a favor. Read that
book for me.

Karen *I* should read it . . . ?

Gould Yes.

Karen The Radiation Book?

Gould Let's be frank: it's probably, it's almost definitely unsuitable, it probably *is* artsy. But as you said, maybe it isn't. *You* read it, you'll tell me, and I'll tell Mr Ross.

Karen ... I ...

Gould ... and then, you're right, and then at least we looked.

Karen I'd be flattered to read it.

Gould *Good.*

Karen Thank you.

Gould Not at all. I thank *you*. I'll need a report on it ...

Karen ... of course.

Gould By tonight. How long will it take you to ...

Karen Well, I won't be able to start reading it 'til after work ...

Gould (*simultaneously with 'work'*) Fine. Tonight, I'm going to be home. When you're finished, you bring the report to me and we'll discuss it.

Karen Absolutely. Thank you.

Gould Not at all. Now, I've ... Please call the Coventry. Tell them, a table for Mr Fox and me, twenty minutes ...

Karen Yes, I will.

Gould I'm going to clean up here before I go. Call Mr Fox's girl up on the phone, get her to *page* him or to try him in the car.

Karen Uh huh.

Gould ... and tell him that I'll be ten minutes late.

Karen Of course ...

Gould ... and tell him he owes me five hundred bucks.

Act Two

Gould's *apartment. Night.* **Gould** *and* **Karen.** **Karen** *is reading from the book.*

Karen He puts his hand on the child's chest, and he says 'heal', as if he felt he had the power to heal him, he calls on God . . . it's in here . . . something to the effect that if *ever* in his life he had the power, any power, that now is the time . . . list . . . (*She reads.*) ' . . . in that lonely place, the low place, the tramp, under the bridge, he finds him. Faced with his troubles, and pours out his heart.' We hear the rain, and we see, in his misery, it is forgotten, wet, cold . . . and the problems which assaulted him: *they do not disappear*, but they are forgotten. He says: years later: it did not occur to him 'til then that this was happiness. That the thing which he lacked, he says, was *courage*. What does the Tramp say? 'All fears are one fear. Just the fear of death. And we accept it, then we are at peace.' And so, you see, and so all of the *events* . . . the *stone*, the *instrument*, the *child* which he met, *led* him there.

Gould They led him.

Karen . . . in his . . . yes, you see – I know that you see – and that's, that's to me, that's the perfection of the story, when I *read* it . . . I almost, I wanted to sit, I saw, I almost couldn't come to you, the *weight* of it . . . (*Pause.*) You know what I mean. He says that the radiation . . . *all* of it, the planes, the televisions, clocks, all of it *is to the one end*. To *change* us – to, to *bring about a change* – all radiation has been sent by God. To change us. Constantly.

Gould To change us.

Karen Yes.

Gould How?

Karen To this new thing. And that we needn't feel frightened. That it comes from God. And I felt empowered. (*Pause.*) Empowered. (*Pause.*)

Gould Empowered...

Karen You've felt that, I hope you've felt that, when something made sense, you'd heard it for the longest time and finally you, you know what it means. So ... so ... it's not *courage*, it's *greater* than courage. Perhaps it *is* courage. You've felt like that.

Gould I have.

Karen Yes.

Gould Felt like...

Karen Like they say in *stories*: where, where one thing changes you.

Gould ... have I felt like that? I don't know.

Karen ... and that it puts you at Peace. And I'll tell you: like books you find at an Inn, or in a bookshop, when, you know, when you go in, that you'll *find* something there, something. Old, or, or scraps of *paper* ... have you had this ...? In a pocket, or, or even on the ground, a phrase ... something that *changes* you. And you were drawn to it. *Just* like the man. Beneath the bridge. 'What was it that you feared?' he says. '*Embrace* it ...' Well! (*Pause.*) And like my coming here. Why? A temporary job. But I thought, who can say I knew, but I thought I knew, I thought: I would find something. (*Pause.*) Too much. It all came at once. So much. May I have another drink? (**Gould** *pours drink.*) Do you know, and he says, the *radiation*, in all things: not just in bombs, in microwaves, in *power*, in *air* travel ... and the *purpose* of this radiation ... well, I've *said* it ...

Gould Thank you.

Karen No, I thank *you*. Do you know what he's talking about? Fear. A life lived in fear, and he says, It Says In The Book, it doesn't have to *be* so; that those things we have *seen* ... *you* know, and you think 'I, am I the only one on the whole planet who knows how *bad* it is ... that it's *coming* ... that it's

sure to come.' What . . . don't you see? What can I do . . . ? And
you *can't* join a convent, or 'cut off your hair', or, or, or, you
see, this is our pain, I think, we *can't* embrace Jesus. *He*, you
see, and he says, 'I know. And you don't have to be afraid.'
And I realized: I haven't *breathed*. How long? In *years*. From, I
don't know. From terror, perhaps ever. And you say, how can
you say it? Is our life so bad? No. No. But that it's ending. That
our life is ending. Yes. It's true. And he says that, that these
are the Dark Ages. (*Pause.*) They aren't to come, the Dark
Ages – they are now. We're living them. (*Reads.*) 'In the
waning days . . . in the last days' . . . 'Yes', he says, it's *true*, and
you needn't deny it . . . and I felt such *fear*, because, of course,
he's right. Then he says: 'do not be afraid.' The story . . . when
you, when you read it, the story itself. Down below the bridge,
I'll tell you: written with such love . . . (*Pause.*) *Such* love . . .
(*Pause.*) God. A thing to be thankful for. Such love.

Gould You've done a fantastic job.

Karen I have?

Gould Yes.

Karen I have? Doing what?

Gould On the book. (*Pause.*)

Karen I . . . ?

Gould In your report on the book. It means something, it
means a lot, I want to tell you, if you want to 'do' something
out here. A *freshness*, you said a *naïveté*, but call it a '*freshness*',
and a capacity to get involved . . . I think that it's fantastic.
And, you know, you dream about making a connection; but I
feel I've *done* it.

Karen You've made a connection . . .

Gould Yes. And you reached out to *me*.

Karen I did . . .

Gould You shared this thing with me.

Karen . . . the book . . .

Gould You did it. Someone does something . . . *totally* . . .

Karen ... yes ...

Gould And you say 'yes' ... '*That's* ... that's what I've been missing.'

Karen ... you're saying ...

Gould That's what I've been missing. I'm saying, you come *alive*, and you see everyone's been holding their *breath* in this town, twenty years, forever, *I* don't know ... and then ...

Karen Yes ...

Gould So rare, someone shows, shows some *enthusiasm* ... it becomes, it becomes *simple*. You know what I mean ...

Karen Yes. I do.

Gould N'I want to thank you. (*Pause.*)

Karen Um ... it's nothing.

Gould (*simultaneously with 'nothing'*) It's something. No. Let, let, let, let me *help* you. That's what I want to do.

Karen (*pause*) I'm confused.

Gould I'm saying I *thank* you; I want to do something for you.

Karen No, no ...

Gould And, whatever, I'm saying, if I can, that you would like to do, in, in the *Studio*, if you would like to do it, if I can help you with it, then I would like to help you.

Karen Yes. *Thank* you. (*Pause.*) I absolutely do. You *know* what I want to do.

Gould I ...?

Karen I want to work on the film.

Gould Alright. If we can. The *Prison* film ...

Karen No. On this. *This* film. The Radiation film and I don't care. I don't care in what capacity, well, why *should* I, 'cause I don't have any skills ... *that's* presumptious, of *course*, in any way I could. But I'd just like, it would be so important to me, to *be* there. To help. (*Pause.*) If you could just help me with that. And, seriously, I'll get coffee, I don't care, but if you could do that for me, I would be ... (*Pause.*)

Gould Hmmm.

Karen I've put you on the spot.

Gould No. Yes, a little.

Karen I'm serious. I'd do *anything* ...

Gould (*pause*) Look ... (*Pause.*) This was a 'courtesy read'.

Karen I know that, but ...

Gould As I told you, the chances were, were astronomically slim that it would ...

Karen Of course, but you said, you, you wanted to *investigate* ...

Gould ... yes ...

Karen ... 'because once in a while' ...

Gould ... yes.

Karen And once in a while one finds a pearl ...

Gould Yes ...

Karen And *this* book ... I'm *telling* you, when you *read* it ...

Gould Karen, it's about the End of the World.

Karen That's what I'm *saying*. That's why it ...

Gould It's about the End of the World.

Karen Uh huh, uh huh. (*Pause.*) This book ... (*Pause.*) This book ... (*Pause.*) But you said someone's job was to read the manuscripts. (*Pause.*)

Gould Someone reads the manuscripts. Yes.

Karen ... that come in ...

Gould ... yes. (*Pause.*) We have readers.

Karen Now: why do the readers read them?

Gould (*simultaneously with 'read'*) I get it. I get it. Yes. As I said. Yes. Once in a while, in a great while, yes, that ...

Karen Why not this? I'm telling you ...

Gould Look: I'm going to pay you the compliment of being frank. (*Pause.*) I'm going to talk to you. (*Pause.*) *Power*, people who are given a slight power, tend to think, they think that they're the only one that has these ideas, pure ideas, whatever, no matter. And, listen to me. Listen. I'm going to tell you. This book. Your book. On The End of the World which has meant so much to you, as I see that it has: Won't Make A Good Movie. Okay? I could tell you many things to influence you. But why? I have to respect your enthusiasm. And I *do* respect it. But this book, you want us to make, won't Get The Asses In The Seats. Sounds crass? Whatever the thing just may be. My job: my job, my new job . . . is not even to 'make', it is to 'suggest', to 'push', to champion . . . good work, I hope . . . choosing *from* Those Things Which the Public Will Come In To See. If they don't come to see it, what's the point? You understand? (*Pause.*) This is what I do. You said a certain kind of courage to embrace a fact? (*Pause.*) This is the fact here.

Karen Why do you . . . (*Pause.*) Your job is to make movies people will come see.

Gould That's right.

Karen Why do you think they won't come see this one? (*Pause.*) Are you ever wrong? Do you see what I'm asking? Just because you think it is 'too good' . . . I . . . I . . . I think they would come see it. (*Pause.*) *I* would. It's about . . . it's about what we feel. (*Pause.*)

Gould It is?

Karen Yes.

Gould Which is . . .

Karen Everyone is frightened.

Gould Everyone is frightened.

Karen Everything is breaking down.

Gould It is?

Karen Yes.

Gould It is?

Karen Yes. It's over . . .

Gould It . . .

Karen I believe it is.

Gould . . . the . . .

Karen . . . things as we know them.

Gould Are over?

Karen Of course they are. Do you see? We don't have to *deny* it . . . The *power* that this thought will release . . . in, in, in *everyone*. Something which speaks to them . . . this book spoke to *me*. It *changed* me . . . I . . .

Gould Yes, but quite frankly the fact that it changed *you*, that *you* like it, that you'd like to see it 'go' is not sufficient reason for the studio to pay fifteen million dollars to put it up there.

Karen A sufficient reason.

Gould Yes.

Karen To make the film.

Gould Yes. (*Pause.*)

Karen Someone, someone makes a decision to, someone can make a decision to . . .

Gould Richard Ross.

Karen You're going to see him tomorrow, you could . . . look. Look, I *read* the script. Mister Fox's script, the prison film. That's, that's just *degradation*, that's the same old . . . it's despicable, it's . . . It's degrading to the human spirit . . . it . . .

Gould It *what* . . . ?

Karen Of course; this rage . . . it's killing people, meaningless . . . the sex, the titillation, violence . . . people don't want, they don't *want*, they . . . they don't want this.

Gould Of course they do, that's what we're in business to do, don't you underst . . . that's what we're in business to do. *Make the thing everyone made last year. Make that image people want to see.* That *is* what they, it's more than what they want. It is what they require. And it's my job. That's my job . . . when I tell Ross about the Douglas Brown film, he's going to fall upon my neck and *kiss* me. *You* know that. *You* know that I can't make this book.

Karen I *don't* know that.

Gould I *told* you . . .

Karen You held out a hope to me, this morning . . .

Gould . . . I held out a hope . . .

Karen . . . that what I said . . .

Gould Aha! You see? That what *you* said . . . We all, as I said, everyone has feelings, *everyone* would like to 'make a difference'. Everyone says 'I'm a maverick' but we're, *you* know that, just one part of the whole, nobody's a maverick.

Karen But . . .

Gould Now: what I told you was: it was a 'courtesy read'.

Karen . . . I, I don't like to be naïve . . .

Gould . . . I told you what the chances were . . .

Karen . . . I don't think it's attractive, and I don't think it's right. To be naïve. But . . .

Gould I *told* you what the deal was. Don't you understand?

Karen But I . . .

Gould But *you*. Yes. Everyone Is Trying To 'Promote' Me . . . Don't you *know* that? Don't you *care*? Don't you *care*? *Every move I make*, do you understand? Everyone *wants* something from me.

Karen (*pause*) Yes. I understand that.

Gould You understand that?

Karen Yes, I do.

Gould Well, if you understand that, then *how can you act this way*?

Karen To come here . . .

Gould Yes.

Karen ... you asked me here. (*Pause.*) I knew what the deal was. I know you wanted to sleep with me. You're right, I came anyway; you're right.

Gould ... to sleep with you ...

Karen Didn't you?

Gould No ...

Karen Why lie? You don't have to lie.

Gould But you're wrong.

Karen But I'm *not* wrong. This is what I'm saying. Are we so *poor* ... that we can't have those simple things: we want love, why should we deny it. Why should you? You could of asked me, you *did* ask me. I know what you meant. That's why I came.

Gould You came to ... ?

Karen I said why not? I'm weak, too. We all need companionship, the things we want ... I wanted them. You're right. I shouldn't act as though I was naïve. I shouldn't act as though I believed you. You're ... but but but:

Gould I asked you here to sleep with me?

Karen Then I read the book. I, I, I've been depraved, too, I've been frightened, I know that you're frightened. I *know* what you are. You see. That's what I'm telling you.

Gould *I'm* frightened ...

Karen I know that you are. I would have come here anyway. Is that depraved? *I* know what it is to be bad. I've been bad, I know what it is to be lost, I know you're lost. *I know* that ... How we are afraid ... to '*ask*', to even '*ask*', and say in jest, 'Yes. I prayed to be pure' ... but it was not an accident. That I came here. Sometimes it reaches for us. And we say 'show me a sign'. And when it reaches us, then we see we *are* the sign. And we find the answers. In the book ...

Gould Why did you say you would come here anyway ...

Karen ... listen to me: The Tramp said 'Radiation'. Well, *whatever* it had been, it makes no difference ... Listen: (*She* *reads*.) 'What was coming was a return to the self, which is to say, a return to God. It was round. He saw all things were round. And the man saw that it all had been devoted to one end. That the diseases in the body were the same diseases in the world. That things were ending. *Yes*. That things *must* end. And that vouchsafed to him a vision of infinity . . . ' You see?

Gould No.

Karen No?

Gould No, I don't understand.

Karen You don't understand.

Gould No.

Karen Would you like to understand? (*Pause*.) The things you've hoped for. The reason you asked me here.

Gould I don't understand you.

Karen You wanted something – you were frightened.

Gould I was frightened?

Karen That forced you to lie. I forgive you.

Gould . . . you forgive me . . . ?

Karen You know how I can? Because we're just the same. You said you prayed to be pure.

Gould I said that . . .

Karen This morning.

Gould I was joking.

Karen I looked in your heart. I saw you. And people can need each other. That's what the book says. You understand? We needn't be afraid.

Gould I don't understand.

Karen You can if you wish to. In the world. Dying. We prayed for a sign. A temporary girl. You asked read the book. I read the book. Do you know what it says? It says that you were put here to make stories people need to see. To make them less afraid. It says in *spite* of our transgressions – that we could do something. Which would bring us alive. So that we

needn't feel ashamed. (*Pause.*) We needn't feel frightened.
The wild animal dies with pride. He didn't make the world.
God made the world. You say that you prayed to be pure.
What if your prayers were answered? You asked me to come.
Here I am.

Act Three

Gould's office. The next morning. **Gould** is sitting behind his desk. **Fox** enters.

Fox Okay. The one, the one, the one thing, I was up all night; I'm sorry, I should be better at these things, I don't know how to say it, you know how you do? You stand and think, you think, and, the only thing, one hand you say: 'Am I worthy to be rich?' The other hand, you, you know, you feel *greedy*; so it's hard to know what's rightfully yours . . . Bob: when we said, when we said: *yesterday*: we were talking, when you said 'producer'; what we *meant*, what we were talking about was, I understand it, that we were to 'share' above-the-title, we would co-produce, because . . . that's right, isn't it? And the other thing; I'm sure you thought of this; to *say* to Ross, to, that we, as a team, you and I, this is only the *beginning*, for, if we brought *this* (I'm sure you thought of this) it's fairly limitless, we can bring *more* . . . those two things, only, what I wanted to say to you . . .

Gould I'm not going to do the film.

Fox Which film?

Gould The Douglas Brown film.

Fox . . . you're not . . .

Gould I'm not going to greenlight the Doug Brown prison film.

Fox I don't blame you. It's a piece of shit. I were you, I'd do the film on Radiation. That's the project I would do. 'A Story of Love, a Story of Hope.' That's what I would do; and then spend the rest of my life in a packing crate. I can't get over those guys. Why do they waste our time? A talky piece of puke. Prestige and all, *okay*, but why, we should just say, 'Sir, Sir, *you* go to the movies . . . if *you* saw a movie of this shit, would you sit through it?' Eastern Office sent the coverage to me – listen to this . . . (*He hunts through his papers. Reads.*) 'The Bridge; or, Radiation, Half-Life and Decay of Society', the Blah Blah . . . set in novel form, The Growth of Radiation, as . . . 'What is this? the device of *God*, in all things, to prepare the world for its final decay.' Yeah. It's a *Summer* picture. (*Pause. Reads again.*) 'The author seems to think that radio and television, aircraft travel and microwaves were invented solely to irradiate the world and so bring about genetic change in humankind.' Great. And Scene Two, he comes out of the bar to find that his horse is gone and he has to go steal the sheriff's nag to ride for help. I'm sorry. I need a drink. Ten o'clock in the morning and I need a drink. You know, you look forward to something and you think it's never going to happen – and you *really* think, bullshit aside, it's never going to happen, and I've got to say, it's *over*, now, yeah, *yeah*, I felt a certain amount of *jealousy*, toward you, here we started out together, and I always said, someday I'll, you know, I'll get something for myself, and it'll be a Brand New Ballgame. I'll sit up there *with* Bobby Gould . . . *over* him . . . you know how we think. Deep inside, I never thought I would. (*Pause.*) And the *other* thing, talk about envy, is, a certain extent, I was riding, several years, on your *coattails* . . . don't say 'no', I know I was, and I want to thank you, that you were *man* enough, that you were *friend* enough, you never brought it *up*, you never rubbed it in. And I'm *glad* I can pay it back. Speaking of paying it back. Do I owe you, for sure, the five c? Fess up. (*Pause.*)

Gould Five c?

Fox The broad come to your house?

Gould The broad?

Fox You fuck the temporary girl? You fuck her. (*Pause.*)

Gould I'm going to go see Ross myself.

Fox You're going to see him yourself. (*Pause.*) Without me, you're saying. (*Pause.*) Do you think that . . . (*Pause.*) Do you think that that's the . . . I mean . . . it was . . . if you think that that's the thing, then that's it. If you think that that's the thing, but, we should, we should, I think we should *talk* about it Bob. Don't you ... (*Pause.*) It was, um, um, uh (*Pause.*) I brought you the picture, Bob.

Gould I know you did.

Fox You see what ... (*Pause.*) I, I, *I* think that we should go in there together. (*Pause.*) Babe. If this is truly a collaborative thing. (*Pause.*) But if you think that ...

Gould I'm not going to take him the Prison Film.

Fox ... if you think that that's the ...

Gould ... are you listening to me? I'm not going to greenlight the pris ...

Fox ... sure, sure, sure ... I understand that, but listen to what I'm asking you. Since I 'brought' ... which, I was saying, since, since I *brought* you the film and since, you say, we're going to split the credit. Because, because what I was *saying*, Bob, to to, finally get a position where I can be *equal*; where *I* brought *you* the film, it means a lot to me, and, frankly, um, um, I think ...

Gould I'm not going to recommend the prison picture.

Fox Okay. (*Pause.*) Is there ... you're not ...

Gould No. (*Pause.*)

Fox I don't understand.

Gould I'm not going to recommend the Doug Brown film. (*Pause.*)

Fox Because ... hold on a second ... hold on a second, before we get to that. You told me yesterday that we were going to go to Ross to greenlight it.

Gould Yes.

Fox You promised me.

Gould I know.

Fox I know that you know. Do you know *why* ...? Because you *did* it.

Gould I know that I did.

Fox You're joking, right?

Gould No. (*Pause.*)

Fox Huh. (*Pause.*) Because, um, you know, I had the package, Doug gave me one day, Doug Brown gave me the one day to have the package, I could have, I could have *took* the thing across the street, you know that? Walked right across the street, As People Do In This Town, and I'd done it *yesterday*, I'd been Executive Producer of a Doug *Brown* film. *Yesterday. Yesterday.* Which is what comes up when you tell me that you aren't going to . . . This is a joke. Right? I'm sorry . . . *I'm* sorry. Bob: When you take the film to Ross . . .

Gould I'm not going to take the film to Ross.

Fox (*pause*) Can you tell me why you're not?

Gould I'm going to greenlight the book.

Fox What book?

Gould The Radiation book.

Fox No, you aren't.

Gould Yes. If I can I am.

Fox I have to siddown. (*Pause.*) Hold on a second, Bob, you're seeing Ross when . . . ?

Gould Twenty minutes.

Fox I'm not upset with you. (*Pause.*) Alright. (*Pause.*) Bob (*Pause.*): Now, listen to me: when you walk in his door, Bob, what you're paid to do . . . now, listen to me now: is make films that make money – you are paid to *make films people like*. And so gain for yourself a *fortune* every day. This is what Ross *pays* us for. This is the thing he and the stockholders want from us. This is what the, listen to me now, 'cause I'm going to 'say' it, Movie Going Public wants from us, excuse me, I'm talking to you like some Eastern Fruit, but *this*, what I've just told you, is your job. You *cannot* make the radiation book.

Gould I'm going to try.

Fox To do something which is right? To do someth . . . ?

Gould I want to read you something. (*Hunts in book. Reads.*)
' "Is it true," she asked, "that we are always in the same state
of growth, the same state of decay as the world in which we
live? If it is true is it not true that the world is then a dream,
and delusion?" All this being true, then what remained to him
was this: Nothing.' (*Pause.*) 'Nothing but God.' (*Pause.*) I've
wasted my life, Charlie. My life is a sham, it's true. But I think
I found something.

Fox Bob, what's happened to you . . . ?

Gould . . . And I think your prison movie has a place . . . and
I respect your . . .

Fox I don't want your respect. Your respect *stinks*: You know
why? You've proved yourself insane. You're gonna buy a
piece of shit . . . you're gonna spend ten million dollars for a
piece of *pussy*, you were 'up all night . . . ' You were up all night
boffing the *broad*. Are you getting *old*? What is this?
Menopause? Your 'life is a sham'? Two days in the new job, you
can't stand the strain . . . ? They're going to invalid you out,
your name will be a *punchline* in this town . . .

Gould . . . if the film doesn't work out here . . .

Fox If the film . . .

Gould The radiation film.

Fox Did you miss your *wake* up call . . . ? If the film doesn't
work out here, you know what you got? Little Lambsy Divey.
No One Will Touch You, do you understand . . . ? You're
throwing your life away. (*Pause.*) Listen to me: Bob (*Pause.*):
Bob (*Pause.*): I have to tell you something . . . It's the
secretary. She, what did she do to you . . . ?

Gould She did nothing to me.

Fox What is she, a witch?

Gould She did nothing, we, we talked . . .

Fox You talked and you decided to throw your career away
. . . ? And my, and my, and *my* chances with it . . .

Gould . . . I don't want . . .

Fox *Bullshit* what you want. *Bullshit*. I Could Of Gone Across the Street.

Gould ... I don't ...

Fox *Fuck* you ... *Fuck* you ... (*He hits* **Gould**.) *Fuck* you. Get up. (*He hits him again*.) I'll fucken' kill you right here in this office. All this bullshit; you *wimp*, you *coward* ... now you got the job, and now you're going to *run* all over everything, like something broke in the *shopping* bag, you *fool* – your fucken' sissy film – you squat to pee. You old *woman* ... all of my life I've been eating your shit and taking your leavings ... *Fuck* you, the Head of Production. Job I could of done ten *times* better'n you, the *press*, the *money*, all this time, and now you're going to be some fucken' *wimp*, cost me my, my, my ... *fortune*? Not In This Life, Pal. Your Writ Has Run. You hear me ...? (*Pause*.) Bob ...? (*Pause*.) Do you hear me ...? You want somebody to take charge? I'll take charge. Do you hear me, mister ...? You need an excuse to cop out, I'll give you your fucken' excuse. (*Pause*.) We have a meeting. Can you fix yourself up?

Gould No. (*Pause*.)

Fox What's the matter?

Gould Nothing.

Fox You have another shirt ...? Can you get through the meeting with Ross?

Gould I'm going to greenlight the radiation book.

Fox It's alright, Bob. It's okay. I see it now. It's okay. Everything is okay. Listen to me, it's alright. I'll explain it to you: a beautiful, a beautiful and an ambitious woman comes to ...

Gould I want you to be careful what you say about her.

Fox It's only words, unless they're true. It's alright, now. I'm sorry I got frightened. Forgive me. I'll explain it to you. (*Pause*.) A beautiful and an ambitious woman comes to town. Why? Why does *anyone* come here ...? You follow my argument? (*Pause*.) Everyone wants power. How do we get it? Work. How do they get it? Sex. The End. She's different?

Nobody's different. *You* aren't, *I'm* not, why should she? The
broad wants power. How do I *know*? Look: She's out with
Albert Schweitzer working in the jungle? No: she's here in
movieland, Bob, and she trades the one thing that she's got,
her *looks*, get into a position of authority – through you.
Nobody likes to be promoted; it's ugly to see, but that's what
happened, babe. I'm sorry. She lured *you* in. 'Come up to my
house, read this script . . . ' She doesn't know what that *means*?
Bob: that's why she's here.

Gould . . . A woman . . .

Fox . . . Hey, pay me the courtesy . . . how *lonely* you must be.
How hard the world is. You complain to her. 'No one
understands me . . . ' '*I* understand you' . . . she says.

Gould She *does* understand me.

Fox Hey, that's *first-rate*.

Gould She *does* understand me . . . she knows what I suffer.

Fox 'What You Suffer . . . '? 'What you suffer . . . '? You're a
whore . . . Bob. You're a *chippy* . . . you're a fucken' bought-
and-paid-for *whore*, and you think you're a ballerina 'cause
you work with your legs? You're a whore. You want some
sympathy? You don't get none. You – you think you can let
down. You *cannot* let down. That's what they pay the big
bucks for. This is what you put up with you wanna have two
homes. Okay? Bob, let's speak frankly, eh? This broad *just took
you down*.

Gould . . . she came to me.

Fox Why did she come to you? 'Cause you're the Baal Shem
Tov? You stupid shit, I'm talking to you . . . Why does she
come to you? 'Cause you're so good looking? She *wants*
something from you. You're nothing to her but what you can
do for her.

Gould You're full of shit.

Fox Uh huh. I know I am.

Gould What does she want from me?

Fox If I'm so smart? She wants you to greenlight this radiation book.

Gould Why?

Fox The fuck should *I* know. *I* don't know. It's not important. Is she Head of Production? *You're* Head of Production. Read the new plaque on your door. Can she greenlight a film? No. *You* can. Now: what does she want from you? Hearth and Home? No. What? Love? Huh? Children? . . . To greenlight a film. To greenlight some bizarre idea . . .

Gould It's not a bizarre idea.

Fox It's not a bizarre idea . . . ? *Tell* it to me . . . Come on. You can't tell it to me in one sentence, they can't put it in TV Guide. What is this movie that you're going to make? Come on, 'A Boy Joins the Cattle Drive and Learns to Be a Man . . .'? 'A Couple Finds a Million Dollars Buried in Their Yard . . .'? Come on, come on . . . what is this movie . . . ? (*Pause.*)

Gould We are . . .

Fox Tell me the story.

Gould We . . . I'm *telling* it to you, and I don't think that we have to mock the possibility that someone could find something that meant something to them. You understand me?

Fox Tell me the film, Bob.

Gould We . . . I'll *tell* you the film. Alright? We are frightened . . . (*Pause.*) Because the World is Ending. Uh . . . (*Pause.*) A man gives up everything . . . wait. (*Pause.*) A man, to find happiness . . . (*Pause.*)

Fox (*picks up the book, reads*) 'A gross infection rampant in the world, they spied, and thought they were the messengers of cure, when they were the disease' . . . (*Turns page and reads again.*) 'That silver is more powerful than gold; and the circle than the square or the triangle. He thought of architecture . . .' (*He throws the book down.*) Are you kidding me . . . ? (*Pause.*) Are you kidding me . . . ? I wouldn't believe this shit if it was *true* . . . the fuck *happened* to you? Let your dick run your *office*? What kind of a man . . .

Gould Okay, Okay. That's enough.

Fox I beg your pardon.

Gould I said that's enough. Get out.

Fox Fuck you.

Gould Fuck me. Fuck me in *hell*. Fuck me in hell, pal. *You* read the plaque on my door. I am your superior. Now, I've made my decision. I'm sorry it hurt you.

Fox It hurt me? You ruined my life.

Gould Be that as it may.

Fox I see.

Gould Now, I have a meeting.

Fox Would you tell me why?

Gould I told you why. Because I've found something that's right.

Fox I can't buy that.

Gould Then 'why' is because I say so.

Fox And eleven years down the drain.

Gould I'm sorry. (*Pause.*)

Fox How sorry are you?

Gould What?

Fox One question . . .

Gould It won't change my mind.

Fox Well then, just say it's a boon, and grant it to me to assuage your guilt. I want to ask your girl one question. Then I swear I'll go.

Gould Alright – ask it.

Fox (*pushes the intercom button; into intercom*) Dear, could you come in here for one moment, please . . . ?

Karen *enters.*

Karen (*to* **Gould**) What *happened* to you?

Fox Where's *Cathy*...?

Karen What happened to you, Bob... are you alr...

Fox Where's Cathy, honey? She still sick...?

Gould It's alright, Karen.

Fox I have one question for you, and then I'll leave you alone. I understand...

Karen I have to... (*Starts to exit.*)

Fox No, no, no, no, no... No, no. It's alright. You alright, Bob?

Gould Yes.

Fox Are you, really, though, *tell* us, now...

Gould I'm fine. We'll be done here in one minute.

Karen What's going on?

Gould Just answer him.

Fox I understand. Karen. I *understand*... that things have been *occurring*... large decisions... do you follow me...? (*Pause.*) Do you follow what I'm going to say?

Karen What do you want?

Fox Well, Dear, I want to ask you something. (*Pause.*)

Karen Alright.

Fox You went to Mister Gould's last night? (*Pause.*)

Karen Yes.

Fox You discussed certain things?

Karen Yes. We did.

Fox You talked about... his new job, you...

Karen You know what we talked about. We *talked* about... we talked about not being frightened. We talked about the ability to make a difference.

Fox To make a difference. Yes.

Karen To make a film...

Fox To make a film that makes a difference. Yes, I know.
Now: listen: I'm not going to talk to you of what gives you the
'insight' to, or the experience to know what will make a good
film. (*Pause.*) I'm not going to ask you, I'm not going to ask
you what, what brought you to this job . . .

Karen . . . it was a temporary job . . .

Fox Uh huh . . . I'm almost there, bear with me. Now: I
understand, last night, that you and Bob became intimate.

Karen I think you should leave.

Fox I know you do, but this is something more than your life,
honey, you're at the Big Table, and, I'm done, then *Bob*, the
Head of Production, is going to say what's what. I have one
question. Now, then, you and Bob, you became 'Lovers'.

Gould Leave her alone.

Fox I don't think so. Do you owe me this? Do you *owe* me this?
For all the years I spent with you? You became *lovers*. (*Pause.*)

Karen Bob? No? Alright. Then, yes. We did.

Fox You talked of love.

Karen Is that . . .

Fox Did . . . ?

Karen Is that so impossible . . . ?

Fox It's not impossible. No. Not at all. You were drawn to
him. You were drawn to a man. It's not impossible, I think
that we would say it happens all the time; you 'said' things to
each other. (*Pause.*) Things occurred. And this is serious.
Forgive me if my words seem to belie that, but I'm doing all I
can, 'cause I love this guy, too. My *question*: you answer me
frankly, as I know you will: you came to his house with the
preconception, you wanted him to greenlight the book.
(*Pause.*)

Karen Yes.

Fox If he had said 'No', would you have gone to bed with
him?

Karen (*pause*) I don't think that I'll answer you.

Fox No?

Karen I don't think you have the right to ask it. Bob . . .

Gould *I* would like to know the answer.

Karen You would.

Gould Yes. I would. (*Pause.*)

Karen Bob. Bob: the man I could respect . . .

Gould Without the bullshit. Just tell me. You're living in a World of Truth. Would you of gone to bed with me, I didn't do your book. (*Pause.*)

Karen No. (*Pause.*) No.

Gould Oh, God, now I'm lost.

Fox Bob . . .

Gould Please be quiet for one moment.

Karen Bob. Bob, we have the opportunity . . .

Fox 'We'? 'We' . . . ? I know who *he* is, who are *you*? Some broad from the Temporary Pool. A Tight Pussy wrapped around Ambition. That's who *you* are, Pal. Now you listen to me, Bob . . .

Gould Charlie. Please . . .

Karen We talked last night, Bob . . .

Gould You told me to Be a Man . . .

Fox 'Be a Man'? 'Be a Man'? What right do you have? You know what this man has *done* . . . ? (*Phone rings,* **Fox** *picks it up. Into phone.*) Yes. One moment. Please . . . (*Hangs up.*)

Gould Oh, God. I don't know what to do.

Fox You know the right thing to do.

Karen Bob, Bob. You reached out to me . . .

Fox He reached out to you? He fucked you on a bet.

Karen I don't care.

Fox You don't 'care'?

Karen Bob, perfect love . . .

Gould Yes. Alright. Alright. Alright. Alright. Perfect Love. Alright. Just *stop* for a moment, will you? Will you? Will you just fuckin' stop taking a *piece* of me for a moment. *Everyone*. Just *stop*. I need one moment, please.

Karen Bob, we decided last *night*.

Gould Yes. I'm *lost*, do you hear me, I'm *lost*. I have to think, I . . .

Karen We decided last night.

Gould We what?

Karen We decided last night.

Fox Bob: I need you.

Gould I have to think.

Fox I need you to remember me.

Gould I have to stop. I have to *think* now.

Karen Bob . . .

Gould . . . No.

Karen Bob, we have a meeting. (*Pause.*)

Fox I rest my case. (*Pause.*)

Karen Did I say something wrong . . . ?

Fox No. We have a meeting, that's true. Thank you, honey.

Karen Did I say something wrong . . . ?

Fox Not at all. (*Picks up phone. Dials.*) Yes. Charlie Fox. Calling for Bob Gould. Mr Gould and I have a . . . Yes. Mr Ross is back from . . . ? Fine. Would you tell him we'll be just two, three minutes late? Thank you. (*Hangs up.*)

Gould I have to change my shirt.

Karen I don't understand.

Gould We're rather busy now. You'll excuse me. Mr Fox will show you out.

Karen No. No. Listen to me. One moment. One moment, Bob. Wait, Bob. The things we said last night. You called for help. Bob, you remember? Listen to me. (*She picks up the book* *and starts to read*.) 'One bell was "showers about us": two bells was "showers across the Lake"; three bells was "showers across the Ocean"; and four bells was "showers across the World". And he wondered how they had obtained that concession to rehearse the bells for the benefit of this instruction.' No, that's the wrong bit. That's not the part ... (**Gould** *exits to the washroom. She looks up*.) Bob ...?

Fox That was a close one. Don't you think?

Karen I think I'm being punished for my wickedness.

Fox Yeah, I do, too. You got a lot of nerve, Babe. And I'll tell you something else, that's why you're *stupid*, is you made your move on something wasn't *ever* going to make a movie. 'Cause the people wouldn't come. (*He picks up the book, reads*.) 'The Earth burned. But the last man had a vision ...'

Karen I don't belong here.

Fox Well, I can help you out on that. You ever come on the lot again, I'm going to have you killed. Goodbye. See you at the A and P.

Karen Goodbye.

Fox I heard you. (*Pause*.)

Karen What did I say ...?

Fox ... Uh huh ...

Karen I don't understand.

Fox I'll send you the coverage. (*Pause*.) Goodbye. You've said your piece. Now go away. (*Pause*.)

Karen I hope ...

Fox We *all* hope. It's what keeps us alive. (*Pause*. **Karen** *exits. He picks up the book, throws it out after her*.) And take this with you. (*To himself*.) 'How are things made round ...' (**Gould** *reenters, tucking in his clean shirt. Pause*. **Gould** *looks at* **Fox**.) Well, Bob, you're human. You think I don't know? I know. We wish people would like us, huh? To Share Our Burdens. But it's not to be.

Gould ... I suppose not.

Fox You're goddamn right, not. And what *if* this fucken' 'grace' exists? It's not for you. You know that, Bob. You know that. You have a different thing.

Gould She told me I was a good man.

Fox How would *she* know? You *are* a good man. Fuck *her*.

Gould I only wanted . . .

Fox I know what you wanted, Bob.

Gould I only wanted . . .

Fox I know what you wanted, Bob. You wanted to do good.

Gould Yes. (*Pause*.) Thank you.

Fox Hey, what'd you want me to say, Bob, you 'Owe' me . . . ? (*Phone rings*, **Fox** *answers it. Into phone*.) We're coming . . . (*Hangs up*.) Because we joke about it, Bob, we joke about it, but it *is* a 'People Business', what else is there . . . ?

Gould I wanted to do Good . . . But I became foolish.

Fox Well, so we learn a lesson. But we aren't here to 'pine', Bob, we aren't put here to *mope*. What are we here to do (*Pause*.) Bob? After everything is said and done. What are we put on earth to do?

Gould We're here to make a movie.

Fox Whose name goes above the title?

Gould Fox and Gould.

Fox Then how bad can life be?